Contents

1

The Quarter

CHESAPEAKE BAY FORMS the western boundary of the section of Maryland which is sometimes called Tidewater Maryland, sometimes called the Eastern Shore. Here there are so many coves and creeks, rivers and small streams, that the land areas are little more than heads or necks of land.

The plantation that belonged to Edward Brodas, in Dorchester County, was typical of this section of Maryland, for one of its land boundaries was a river—the Big Buckwater River. The nearest village, Bucktown, was little more than a settlement composed of post office, church, crossroads store, and eight or ten dwelling houses.

Edward Brodas was known as the Master to his slaves. His house, which the slaves called the Big House, stood near a country road. The kitchen was a small detached building in the rear, known as the cookhouse. Not too far away from the Big

House were the stables, where the riding horses and the carriage horses, the grooms and the hostlers were housed. Close to the stables were the kitchen gardens and the cutting gardens. Beyond these lay the orchards and the barns.

Out of sight of the Big House, but not quite out of hearing, was the "quarter" where the slaves lived.

The quarter consisted of a group of one-room, windowless cabins. They were built of logs that had been cut from nearby forests. These rough-hewn logs were filled with sap, and as they dried out the roofs sagged, the walls buckled. The narrow clay-daubed chimneys leaned as though some unseen pressure were forcing them over.

The cabins were exactly alike inside, too. There was a crude fireplace with one or two black iron pots standing in front of it. The hearth was merely a continuation of the dirt floor. When the wind blew hard, smoke came down the chimney in puffs, so that the walls were smoke-darkened.

Harriet Greene, who was usually called Old Rit, and her husband, Benjamin Ross, both slaves, lived in one of these windowless cabins, on the Brodas plantation. They had several children, some of whom still lived with them.

In 1820, Old Rit had another baby. There was no record made of the date of the birth of this child, because neither Old Rit nor her husband, Ben, could read or write.

Old Rit and Ben decided that they would call this new baby Araminta, a name that would be shortened to Minta or Minty. This would be her basket name or pet name, and would be used until she grew older. Then they would call her Harriet. That year would be separated from the others as "the year Minty was born."

News, good or bad, traveled swiftly through the quarter. All the slaves knew that Old Rit had another baby. That night they left their own cabins, moving like shadows, pausing now and then to listen for the sound of hoofbeats along the road, a sound that meant the patrollers were hunting another runaway. Only they added an extra syllable to the word, making it "patteroller." Then, moving quietly, quickly, they slipped inside Ben's cabin, to look at the new baby.

They arrived in groups, two or three at a time, and stood looking down at the baby. They admired it, briefly. They asked after the mother's health, and then lingered on, squatting down in front of the open fire, talking. The talk around the fire was about the new overseer, about the corn crop, about the weather, but it ended with the subject of freedom—just as it always did.

The bold ones, young, strong, said freedom lay

to the North, and one could obtain it if one could but get there. A hush fell over the cabin, an uneasiness entered the room. It seemed to reach the sleeping children, huddled on the old blankets in the corner, for they stirred in their sleep.

They were all silent for a moment, remembering the ragged, half-starved runaways that they had seen brought back in chains, branded with an R, remembering how they had seen them whipped and sent South with the chain gang.

Then another of the slaves broke the silence. He used a long word: manumission. It was a word the master used. It was a promise that had been made to all of them. If they were faithful and hardworking, the master would set them free, manumit them, when he died.

One of the sad dispirited slaves said that freedom lay only in death.

The bold ones said this was not true. They said you could run away, get to the North and be free. Slaves were disappearing all the time from the nearby farms and plantations. True, some of them were caught, brought back and sold South, but many of them were not. Quite often the masters and the overseers came back without the runaways. Surely some of them must have reached the North.

When the slaves learned that they were to be sold, they ran away. They always knew when the decision had been reached to sell them. They were afraid of the living death that awaited them on the rice fields, cotton plantations, and sugar plantations in the deep South—and so ran away.

To the slaves those words, sold South, sold down the river, carried the sound of doom. The master used it as a threat to recalcitrant slaves. The runaways that were caught and brought back were immediately sold South, as a punishment for running away.

Thus the action on both sides was like a circle that went around and around, never ending. The master kept selling slaves because he needed money. The slaves, learning that they were about to be sold, would run away. The number of runaways from Maryland kept increasing. Especially from this Eastern Shore where the rivers and coves offered a direct route to the North.

That night in the quarter, one of the bold young slaves said if one could get hold of a boat, and there were boats everywhere—rowboats, gunning skiffs, punts—one could get away.

2

The First Years

LIKE ALL THE OTHER BABIES in the quarter, Harriet Ross cut her first teeth on a piece of pork rind. The rind was tied to a string, and the string hung around her neck.

She learned to walk on the hard-packed earth outside the cabin, getting up, falling down, getting up again—a small naked creature, who answered to the name of Minta or Minty.

When she finally mastered the skill of walking, she began playing with other small children. All of the little ones were placed under the care of a woman, so old she could no longer work. She was a fierce-looking old woman, head wrapped in a white bandanna which she called a head rag. She sat on the doorstep of her cabin, sucking on an empty clay pipe.

The mothers of these children worked in the

fields. A few of them, like Old Rit, worked in or around the Big House.

Because the mothers were not at home, a family rarely ate together, all at the same time. The grownups ate from the skillet or black iron pot in which the food was cooked. Some of them ate from tin plates, balanced on the knees, eating for the most part with their hands.

The children were fed in a haphazard fashion, a bit of corn bread here, a scrap of pork there; occasionally they received a cup of milk, sometimes potatoes.

Harriet, like the rest of the children, learned quickly that he who ate the fastest, got the most food. Yet they were always a little hungry, not starving, but with an emptiness inside them that was never quite assuaged.

She learned other things, too. On winter days, when the sun shone, she played on the south side of the cabin, where it was warmer. On cold rainy days, she huddled in a corner of the big chimney in the cookhouse, watching the constant stirring of the big iron pots. In the summer, when the sun was blistering hot, she stayed on the north side of the cabin because it was cooler there.

There was fear and uneasiness all over the South that year. Fear on both sides. The masters were afraid of the slaves. The slaves were afraid of the masters.

Yet the slaves had to talk about this new and dreadful thing that had happened.

Denmark Vesey was a free black man. He bought his freedom when he was thirty-three. He had been a sailor. He could read and write. He was always reading the Bible. He told and re-told the story of the children of Israel, and how they escaped from bondage, to a group of slaves who were his followers. He told them that all men were born equal. Finally, he planned an insurrection, in which he and his followers were to kill all the white people in Charleston, South Carolina, and free the slaves.

He had two men who worked closely with him, who helped him make the homemade pikes that were used in the insurrection. These men were Peter Poyas and Mingo Harth. They kept lists of the names of Denmark's followers, of the places where ammunition was kept, places where there were horses, and the names of slaves who looked after horses.

Two days before this uprising was to take place, the plot was revealed. One hundred thirty-one slaves, in and around Charleston, were ar-rested. Denmark and thirty-four others were hanged. None of them confessed. The story went that Peter Poyas said, "Die silent," when one of the slave conspirators appeared to be weakening under torture.

There were new laws now, because of Denmark. The new laws took away what little freedom of movement they had had. A slave caught on the road, alone, without a pass, would be whipped. Not by the overseer, or the master, but by any white man who happened to see him.

They were not supposed to talk to each other either. Two slaves standing talking would be whipped. They might be plotting servile insurrection, those long hard words that meant death to the master, death to the slave, too.

Night after night they slipped into each other's cabins and talked of the man Denmark Vesey, of freedom, of the children of Israel and how they were led out of bondage.

Old Rit did not like all this talk of freedom and of Denmark Vesey. She said that the master had promised to free her and Ben and the children when he died. There was hope in her voice, mixed with fear. Because the master might forget to write it down in his will.

Like the rest of the slaves, she feared change. She liked this place where they lived. The older children worked on nearby farms, so they were still together, as a family. True, the cabin was hot in summer, and filled with cold drafts in the winter, and the smoke from the fireplace half blinded them, but it was still a good place—it was their home.

The master thought well of her and of Ben. Ben was big, broad-shouldered, a valuable hand. He worked in the woods, felling trees. She some-times teased him about his ax. He was as fond of it as though it were a person. He said it was just right, it fitted his hands, almost worked by itself.

Ever since the slaves started all this talk about Denmark Vesey, she had been uneasy, insecure. She worried about the children. They would never be really hers until they were free. Yet free-dom was a dangerous thing to even think about. She wished the slaves would stop whispering about it all the time.

But every night, before these whispered con-versations came to an end, one of the bolder slaves spoke of Denmark Vesey, voice pitched low, not much more than a murmuring in the firelit cabin. He talked about the slave who protested when Denmark had said that all men were equal. The slave had said, "But we are slaves." Den-mark Vesey had said, "You deserve to be."

Six Years Old

By the time harriet ross was six years old, she had unconsciously absorbed many kinds of knowledge, almost with the air she breathed. She could not, for example, have said how or at what moment she learned that she was a slave.

At the same time, someone had taught her where to look for the North Star, the star that stayed constant, and told her that anyone walking toward the North could use that star as a guide.

She knew about fear, too. Sometimes at night, or during the day, she heard the furious galloping of horses. She saw the grown folks freeze into stillness, not moving while they listened. She could not remember who first told her that those furious hoofbeats meant the patrollers were going past, in pursuit of a runaway. Only the slaves said patterollers, whispering the word.

Thus Harriet already shared the uneasiness

and the fear of the grownups. But she shared their pleasures, too. She knew moments of pride when the overseer consulted Ben, her father, about the weather. Ben could tell if it was going to rain, when the first frost would come, whether there was going to be a stretch of clear sunny days. Everyone on the plantation admired this skill of Ben's. Even the master, Edward Brodas.

The other slaves were rather in awe of Ben. All through the plantation, from the Big House to the fields, he had a reputation for absolute honesty. He had never been known to tell a lie. He was a valued worker and a trusted one.

Ben could tell wonderful stories, too. So could her mother, Old Rit, though Rit's were mostly from the Bible. Rit told about Moses and the children of Isreal, about how the sea parted so that the children walked across on dry land, about the plague of locusts, about the long journey to the Promised Land.

Old Rit taught Harriet the words of that song that the slaves were forbidden to sing, because of the man named Denmark Vesey, who had urged the other slaves to revolt by telling them about Moses and the children of Israel. Sometimes, in the quarter, Harriet heard snatches of it, almost whispered: ''Go down, Moses. . . .''

She was aware of all these things and many

other things too. She learned to separate the days of the week. Sunday was a special day. There was no work in the fields. The slaves cooked and washed their clothes and sang and told stories.

There was another special day, issue day, which occurred at the end of the month. It was the day that food and clothes were issued to the slaves. Men and women received a coarse blanket apiece. The children kept warm as best they could.

And so Harriet knew about Sunday which came once a week, about issue day which occurred once a month. She learned to divide time into larger segments too, based on changes of the season. There was seedtime when warmth began to creep back into the land. This was followed by the heat of summer. Then heat lay over the fields like a blanket; the bent backs of the field hands glistened in the sun, black backs wet with sweat.

After the heat of summer, the year turned toward the fall, the nights began to grow cooler. Then came harvest, one of the best times of the year, when the big full moon lit the fields and the slaves worked late, singing songs like a thanksgiving for the abundance of the crop.

Harriet thought that Christmas was the very best time of all. By tradition there was no work. The holiday for the field slaves lasted as long as the Yule log burned in the fireplace at the Big House. So the people in the quarter spent days preparing the log. They chose a big one and soaked it in water, so that it would burn slowly and for a long time.

It was cold at Christmastime, cold in the winter there on the Eastern Shore. Yet Harriet liked the winter. She watched the flickering light from the fire. It cast long dancing shadows against the smoke-darkened walls. She knew and liked the damp earthy smell of the dirt floor, even though they slept on the floor, aware of the chill.

At night, inside the cabin, she felt safe. But with the coming of morning, she was always a little frightened. In the early morning dark, she heard and recognized the long low notes of the overseer's horn, calling the field hands to work.

And so at six, Harriet already knew fear and uneasiness. She knew certain joys too, the joy of singing, the warmth from a pine-knot fire in a fireplace, the flickering light that served as deco-ration, making shadows on the walls, changing, moving, dancing, concealing the lack of furniture.

Hired Out

IN THE SUMMER OF 1826, Harriet was six years old and, by plantation standards, big enough to work. She carried water to the field hands, and listened to their rhythmical singing, watched how the movement of their hands, their bodies, was paced to the rhythm of the song.

That year, in the fall, a woman drove up to the Big House in a wagon. She went inside and stayed for quite a while. Almost as soon as she arrived, word of what she wanted was relayed through the quarter.

This woman had come to see the master. She wanted to hire one of the master's slaves, preferably a girl, and young, because she couldn't pay very much.

Before six-year-old Harriet knew what was happening, she was seated in the wagon, beside this strange white woman who was now her mistress. She had been "hired out" by the master. Mrs. James Cook was going to pay him a small sum a month for the services of Harriet.

When the wagon finally stopped near a house, Harriet was disappointed in it. It was not like the Big House. It was built of logs, just like the cabins in the quarter. But at least it was near a river, though she never knew the name of the river.

Mrs. Cook was a weaver. She spent most of the day in front of a big loom, head bent, arms moving back and forth. Harriet was supposed to help her. She stood for hours, winding yarn, her hands clumsy, unaccustomed to the job, the thread catching on the rough places on her fingers.

She hated the inside of the house. She slept in the kitchen, in a corner near the fireplace; toward morning, when the fire went out, she slept with her feet tucked under the warm ashes because it was so cold at night. The people fed her scraps of food, much as they might have fed a dog.

The woman said Harriet was clumsy, slow, no help at all, so the man set her to watching his trap lines. He had his traps set for muskrats.

One morning she woke up coughing, eyes watering, feeling sick, hot, utterly miserable. Mrs. Cook said that slaves were always pretending to be sick in order to avoid work, that young as Minty was, she too had learned to slack off.

So James Cook sent Minty out to inspect his

trap lines. She stumbled along, head down, vision blurred by the watering of her eyes. She wasn't crying—but her eyes kept filling up with tears. The water in the river was so cold that she shuddered as she waded along the edge. She had to wade to see if the traps had been sprung. She bent over, shivering, examining a trap, not liking the scaly look of the tails of the muskrats and yet not liking to see them caught in the traps.

When she went back to the house, a small bent-over figure, shivering and shaking, it was obvious that she was really sick. Mrs. Cook got a blanket and threw it over her, wondering audibly what was wrong with Minty.

She was so sick that Old Rit heard about it, and went to Edward Brodas and asked him to take Minty away from Cook's, to let her come home. The master consented.

Rit nursed Harriet back to health. It was six weeks before she was really well. She had the measles. Because of the wading in the cold river, she developed bronchitis. Rit kept giving her a hot and bitter brew, made from the root of a plant that Ben brought back from the woods.

There was always a huskiness in Harriet's voice after that. It stayed there for the rest of her life, an undertone that lent an added timbre to her voice.

As soon as Harriet recovered, the master sent

her back to the house of James Cook. When Minta, or Minty, whose Christian name was Harriet, went back to the Cooks, she soon learned that she was to stay indoors and learn to weave. She was not to walk Cook's trap lines any more.

She felt like the muskrats. One moment she had seen them diving and swimming in the river, and then suddenly click, and they were caught fast in the trap. She remembered that some of them had fought to free themselves, tearing fur and flesh to get free.

She decided that she simply would not learn to weave. She hated being inside the house with the loom and the spinning wheel and the endless hanks of yarn. There was always lint in the air. She was always cold. She did not get enough to eat. She wanted to go home.

And so, finally, Cook's wife sent Harriet back to the Brodas plantation. She said that she was unteachable, intractable, hopelessly stupid.

Flight

ONCE AGAIN, HARRIET, the small girl in the tow-linen shirt, barefooted, feet not touching the floor of the wagon, sat listening to the clop-clop of horses' hoofs, listening to the creak of a wagon that was carrying her farther and farther away from home.

Finally the wagon stopped in front of a big house. She never did know where it was located, near what town, how far away from the Brodas plantation. But she soon knew what she was supposed to do. She looked after Miss Susan's baby and helped with the housework, too. It wasn't a big family, just Miss Susan and her husband, and the baby, and Miss Emily, a sister of Miss Susan's who was visiting.

That first morning, Miss Susan told her to go and sweep the parlor and dust it. She swept as hard as she could, and then immediately dusted all the dark shiny wood of the furniture.

Miss Susan said, "Have you finished?" and came in to run her fingers over the shiny surface of the chairs and tables. Her fingers were coated with dust. "Do it again," she snapped. "Are you just plain stupid? Why, you haven't dusted in here at all. You do it right—or—"

Harriet swept again, and then dusted, getting more and more frightened. Miss Susan said it wasn't done properly and went and got a whip and kept whipping her and shouting at her; and Harriet screamed.

Miss Emily had heard the screams and came downstairs, protesting, "Why do you whip the child, Susan, for not doing what she has never been taught to do? Leave her to me a few minutes, and you will see that she will soon learn how to sweep and dust a room."

Harriet learned how to clean the house. She looked after the baby, too. In later life, she said, "I was so little that I had to sit on the floor and have the baby put in my lap. That baby was always in my lap except when it was asleep or its mother was feeding it."

Miss Susan said that the baby mustn't be allowed to cry. Harriet had to keep rocking it so it wouldn't cry. Every night the same thing happened. She sat on the floor and rocked the cradle back and forth, back and forth, until the baby went to sleep. Then her head drooped, her eyelids closed, her hand started slipping, slipping, slipping from the dark polished wood of the cradle. Finally she slept, on the floor by the cradle.

Then the baby would wail, suddenly, a thin, high, piercing sound. Miss Susan would wake up, furious, and reach for the whip she kept on a little shelf behind her bed.

Harriet finally reached a point in exhaustion where she was past needing sleep, where she snatched it in brief moments, head nodding, eyes closed, and yet not really asleep, prepared to start rocking the cradle before the baby woke up and cried.

She thought of running away, and didn't. She did not know how to reach the Brodas plantation, did not know in which direction to walk, assuming that she could have got away from the house. She had no idea how far it was. It had seemed an interminable journey when the overseer brought her to Miss Susan's in a wagon.

During the day, she toyed with the idea of running away. Then she would thrust the thought from her as impossible.

Yet she did run away. Years afterward, she described what happened in these words: ''One morning, after breakfast, Miss Susan had the baby, and I stood by the table waiting until I was to take it; near me was a bowl of lumps of white sugar. My mistress got into a great quarrel with her husband; she had an awful temper, and she would scold and storm and call him all kinds of names.

"Now you know, I never had anything good, no sweet, no sugar; and that sugar, right by me, did look so nice, and my mistress's back was turned to me while she was fighting with her husband, so I just put my fingers in the sugar bowl to take one lump and maybe she heard me for she turned and saw me.

"The next minute she had the rawhide down. I give one jump out of the door and I saw that *they* came after me, but I just flew and *they* didn't catch me. I ran and I ran and I passed many a house, but I didn't dare to stop for they all knew my mistress and they would send me back."

She ran until she was exhausted. She kept looking over her shoulder. After a while she didn't see Miss Susan and her husband. She decided that they must have got tired and stopped chasing her. She slowed her pace, then at the thought of having to go back to Miss Susan and whatever form of punishment she and her husband would have devised, she started running again.

She said, "By and by when I was almost tuckered out, I came to a great big pigpen. There was an old sow there, and perhaps eight or ten little pigs. I was too little to climb into it, but I tumbled over the high part and fell in on the ground; I was so beaten out that I could not stir.

"And there I stayed from Friday until the next Tuesday, fighting with those little pigs for the potato peelings and the other scraps that came down in the trough. The old sow would push me away when I tried to get her children's food, and I was awfully afraid of her. By Tuesday I was so starved I knew I had to go back to my mistress. I didn't have anywhere else to go, even though I knew what was coming. So I went back."

6

The Underground Road

HARRIET WAS BACK on the Brodas plantation, back in the slave quarter. Miss Susan brought her back and told the master that Minta wasn't "worth a sixpence."

Old Rit sniffed her contempt for Miss Susan when she saw Minta. The child was little better than skin and bones. She was as filthy as though she'd been living in a hog wallow, and her neck and back were covered with scars, old scars crisscrossed with fresh ones from the beating Miss Susan and her husband had given her because she ran away.

It was slow work, but Old Rit got the fresh scars healed up, and then when Harriet began to get a little flesh on her bones, Brodas hired her out again.

In a way, Harriet had won a victory—though Rit did not think so. Harriet worked in the fields from then on. Brodas hired her out to a man who kept her out of doors. She loaded wood on wagons, split rails, and knew more about mules and hoes and plows than she did about the interior of a house. Despite her strong sturdy body, she was still a child. Yet she was often ordered to perform jobs that would have taxed the strength of a full-grown, able-bodied man. If she failed in any of these backbreaking jobs, she was beaten.

Her appearance began to change. The solemn-eyed, shy little girl, hesitant of speech, had disappeared. She was replaced by a sullen-eyed creature, the lids hanging heavily over the eyes. She had the calloused work-hardened hands of a field slave.

She worked from dawn to dusk, worked in the rain, in the heat of the sun. Her muscles hardened. She sang when she was in the fields or working in the nearby woods. Her voice was unusual because of the faint huskiness. Once having heard it, people remembered it.

That year, 1831, Harriet kept hearing a strange, fascinating story in the quarter, in the fields. This same story about a slave named Tice Davids was being told in the Big House, too. But with a difference. The slaves told it with relish, the masters with distaste.

Tice Davids ran away from his master in Kentucky. He planned to cross the Ohio River at Ripley. But his master followed so close behind him that Tice had to jump in the river and swim across.

The master never saw Tice Davids again. He combed the countryside; he searched the anti-slavery town of Ripley. He knew that the town had a reputation of being hostile to slaveholders, had heard vaguely of a Reverend John Rankin who served as watchdog and guardian of run-aways—Even so. Tice Davids had disappeared right before his master's eyes.

The master went back to Kentucky and told about this strange disappearance, how his slave, Tice, had literally vanished before his eyes. Puzzled, disturbed more than he cared to admit, he explained this mystery by saying, "He must have gone on an underground road."

Harriet was puzzled by this story. She kept thinking about it. Was there a road that ran under the ground? Was that how Tice Davids had escaped from his master? If Tice could find it, could other people find it, too?

People in the border states, who had been sheltering runaway slaves, helped further the mystery of an underground road. The new steam trains were being talked about everywhere. A rumor started, and spread, to the effect that there was an underground railroad too.

The free blacks, the Quakers, the Methodists, the German farmers, who helped runaway slaves Ohio, Pennsylvania, New York, started using phrases and words suited to the idea of a railroad. They called themselves conductors, stationmasters, brakemen. Their houses and barns and haystacks, and the unsuspected secret passages inside the big farmhouses, were called depots and stations. They referred to the runaways as passengers, parcels, boxes, bales of black wool. Large parcels were grown-ups; small parcels were children.

This mysterious underground railroad was spoken of, in whispers, in the quarter on the Brodas plantation, just as it was on all the other plantations.

In that same year, in August, in October, in November, the slaves in the quarter and the masters in the Big Houses began to talk about another story. In the quarter, the name of the man who was involved was never spoken aloud. It was always whispered, as though the land, the trees, the sky, the rivers and coves had ears. For this was a horror story. Its details were known all over the United States. Like the other slaves, Harriet knew the story as accurately and as completely as though she had been an eyewitness to the event.

It was the story of Nat Turner. He was a slave, in Southampton, Virginia. He was called The Prophet. He was a preacher.

On the night of August 20, 1831, he said to six of his followers: "Our race is to be delivered from bondage, and God has appointed us as the men to do His bidding; I am told to slay all the whites we encounter, men, women and children . . . it is necessary that in the commencement of this revolution all the whites we meet must die."

They set out together, Nat Turner and his six followers, and at every plantation where they stopped, other slaves joined them, until there were seventy of them altogether. They killed sixty white persons, men, women and children, found on plantations within a radius of twenty miles.

The local militia and Federal troops were called in to quell this unplanned and unrehearsed insurrection. All through the South, slaveholders were terrified. Though one hundred slaves were killed in the process of putting down this revolt, Nat Turner could not be found. He stayed hidden in a cave in Southampton County for two months. He was finally found, and executed on November 11, 1831.

After the Nat Turner insurrection, fear hung over the plantations from Virginia on down through Maryland, down to Louisiana, Alabama, Mississippi. The slave-holders lived in dread because the most faithful house slave might at any moment become another Nat, attacking the master, in the dead of night, with no warning.

New laws were passed in the slave states and the old laws were more rigidly enforced. Nat Turner had been a silent, brooding slave. Get rid of the silent ones. He had been a preacher, he had talked about the children of Israel, about Moses—therefore there must be no more Sunday schools for children who were slaves, no more separate church services for the slaves. They must not be permitted to congregate anywhere, at any time. Must not be allowed to talk freely to each other. Under no circumstances must they be permitted to learn to read and write. Make it a crime for anyone to teach them.

7

"Shuck This Corn"

IT WAS THE FALL of the year. The corn and wheat were being harvested. The harvesting of the corn was, traditionally, the occasion for rejoicing. The days were getting shorter, the nights were perceptibly cooler, the year was turning toward the Christmas season and the long holiday which the entire countryside would celebrate.

In the fields, late in the day, afternoon merging into night, a cornhusking bee was in progress on the Brodas plantation. The corn had been stacked in a great mound. The master had invited his friends to send their slaves to help shuck the corn.

The slaves had mounded the corn up, higher, higher, higher, dark hands lifting the ears of corn, slight rustle from the ears, two or three hundred slaves moving around the great stack.

One of Barrett's slaves stood silent at the foot of the big pile of corn. Harriet watched him, aware that the overseer was watching him, too. A silent slave was not liked by overseers, because a silent slave was probably brooding about escape or revolt. He might have persuaded the others to take part in whatever it was that he was plotting. He might be another Denmark Vesey or Nat Turner—She watched him and felt a prickle of fear run through her.

The slaves set to work husking the corn, racing with each other, to see who could husk the most in the shortest possible time. They started singing a song, its tempo faster and faster, the movement of their hands paced to the rhythm of the song, and the sound of the rustling of the husks of the corn like an accompaniment.

Harriet watched Barrett's slave, her own hands moving swiftly, stripping the husks from the corn, enjoying the fading light, the coolness that lay over the land, the look of the cornfield now that the crop was harvested, and working, and yet watching the big young man who stood silent, whose hands moved slowly, desultorily.

She leaned over to pick up an ear of corn, and when she looked for him, he was moving away. His swiftly moving figure was in strange contrast to the languorous slow motion of his hands just a few minutes before.

The overseer did not see him until he was

halfway across the field. He called to him, ordering him to come back. The big young man kept going, faster now. The overseer followed him, the black-snake whip in his hand.

Harriet went too. There would be trouble. She knew there was going to be trouble, she could always tell when it was coming, by the peculiar fluttering of her heart. It was a warning signal, and it was telling her now that something dreadful was going to happen.

They went down one of the old rolling roads, the slave running, and the overseer running too. He had not expected trouble in the middle of a husking bee, an occasion for frolicking and fun. Harriet followed close behind.

The slave ducked inside the door of the store at the crossroads. The overseer went after him. Harriet heard him say that he would whip him right then and there, and thus teach him not to run away from his work. He called for help, to tie the slave. He ordered Harriet to help told him.

She did not move. She stood there just inside the door watching these two. The overseer could not hope to whip the slave unless someone helped tie him up. The big young man who belonged to Barrett dodged past the overseer, head down, and was through the door and gone—just that fast.

Runaway slaves who were caught were whipped, branded, and brought back in chains. Young Harriet Tubman lay awake at night listening for the hoofbeats of patrollers' horses.

Harriet moved in front of the doorway, stood there, blocking it. The overseer, startled by this sudden obstructing body, planted squarely in the doorway, turned away from the door, picked up a two-pound weight from the counter, and hurled it at the fleeing slave.

The weight missed the slave. It struck Harriet in the forehead, leaving a great open gash there. She was thrown backward from the force of the blow. She was brought back to the quarter, unconscious, bleeding.

In the quarter the slaves came to look at her. They said that she would surely die. No one could survive with a great hole in the head like that, the life's blood draining out.

Old Rit nursed Harriet alone, unaided. She even called in the old man that they said could conjure, though she doubted that any conjurer in the world could save this child. At night, in the flickering light from the fire, the wound, that great hole in the forehead, throbbed.

The cornhusking was forgotten, the fun of it, the singing, the capering that had gone on while they husked the corn.

November came and passed. Then it was Christmas. Harriet was in a stupor most of the time, deaf to the laughter, the dancing and the singing.

Right after Christmas the overseer began again, trying to sell her. Neighboring farmers came and looked at her and snorted their refusal to buy her; some of them laughed and said Brodas was crazy to try to sell such a wreck; others said he would have to pay them to take her off his hands, not worth a sixpence—sell her?

Harriet stayed in the cabin from Christmas until March, and toward the end of this long period of inertness, she began to pray for the conversion of Edward Brodas, repeating the same prayer, over and over again, "Change his heart, Lord, convert him."

In March, too, when it was obvious that she was getting better, she learned that she and her brothers were to be sold South, part of the next chain gang. Austin Woodfolk, the slave trader, was in Cambridge, and Brodas had arranged for her sale.

The knowledge that she would be sold terrified her. There was always an ache in her skull, a pounding. The wound had healed but it was still painful. She was subject to violent headaches. What was worse, she never knew at what moment she would suddenly go to sleep. It was as though she lost consciousness. She never knew when this would happen or for how long a period of time. When she slept like that, she could not be roused. It was like a coma. She could remember what had gone on just before the period of unconsciousness, could pick up a conversation, the threads of it. If she was talking herself when she suddenly went to sleep, she would finish whatever she was going to say when she awakened.

But she was going to be sold. She changed the prayer that she said every night. She no longer prayed for the master's conversion. She said, ''Lord, if you're never going to change that man's heart—*kill him*, Lord, and take him out of the way—''

''*Kill him*, Lord,'' she prayed. She knew she couldn't run away. She might be found sound asleep, not a mile away from the plantation, motionless by the side of the road, in plain view.

A few days later she heard that Edward Brodas, the master, was sick, and that the doctor had told the family he would surely die.

And then, suddenly, one morning the master was dead. The field hands knew he was dead before the overseer knew it. And no one watching them could really have said how the news spread so fast, the length and breadth of the whole plantation, though the word went from the master's bedroom, to the kitchen, then to the stable, then to the quarter, where the little children managed to tell the field hands while they brought the water to them.

It was planting time, and the backs of the field hands were bent as they leaned over the long rows, sun glistening on their bare backs. Seedtime. Seedtime.

The overseer, a man on horseback watching them, suddenly shouted, "Make a noise there!" because a hush fell over the field.

They began to sing. But it was a slow-moving song, pitched higher than anything he had ever heard, with a wail in it that made him shiver.

Old Rit told Harriet that the master was dead. She didn't need to tell her. When Harriet heard that long slow wail from the fields, she knew he was dead. She lay on the floor of the cabin, motionless, conscience-stricken, filled with horror. She believed that her prayers had killed him.

Minta Becomes Harriet

THERE WAS PANIC in the quarter. The master was dead. Would the slaves be sold? Would all these families be separated and scattered about the countryside? The older slaves whispered to each other, saying: "Did he free us as he promised?"

The slaves were quickly reassured. The overseer told them that the plantation was to remain intact. It had been willed to an heir who was too young to administer it. It would be managed by the young master's guardian, Dr. Anthony Thompson, a minister in Bucktown. According to the master's will, none of the slaves could be sold outside the state of Maryland.

This information ended the whispered, panicky conversations in the quarter. It did nothing to end Harriet's feeling of guilt.

She was uneasy, too. She knew that she was no longer regarded as a desirable slave. There was always the possibility that Dr. Thompson, once he heard the story of the way in which she had defied an overseer, would decide to sell her.

Once again she toyed with the idea of running away. Somehow the urgency was gone. Old Rit and Ben were here on the plantation. So were her brothers and sisters. All of them had joyously accepted the announcement that nothing was to be changed.

But who could be certain? The master had promised to free Old Rit, but he hadn't. He had never been cruel to his slaves. But he hired them out to men who were cruel. He sold them whenever the need arose. He had tried to sell her when she was sick and worthless. No one could know what this temporary master, Doc Thompson, as he was known in Bucktown, would be like.

After the terrible wound in her head had healed, she became aware of the admiration of the other slaves. Even the old ones listened to her opinions, deferred to her. Though Old Rit continued to deplore the audacity, the boldness in Harriet that made her defy an overseer, she stopped calling her Minta or Minty. So did the others.

She was Harriet now to all of them. It was as though the pet names were no longer suitable for a teen-aged girl who bore on her forehead a great scar, irradicable evidence of the kind of courage rarely displayed by a grownup.

Though the wound in her head had healed, she was subject to periods of troubled sleep, she had strange dreams which recurred night after night. These dreams had a three-dimensional quality in which people and places were seen more clearly than in her waking moments. At night, in the quarter, she described these dreams or visions, as she called them, to the other slaves. Even in the telling, the reality of the dream came through to the others, so that they were awed by her.

As soon as she was able to work again, Doc Thompson hired out Harriet and her father, Ben, to John Stewart, a builder. At first Harriet worked in his house, doing the housework.

There was no question but what she was well enough to work, though she sometimes had severe headaches, especially if she got very tired. The headaches did not bother her as much as the sudden onset of that deep trancelike sleep which still occurred without warning.

After three months of housework, she asked Stewart, her temporary master, if she could work in the woods with the men. Stewart knew she was strong. He had seen her bring in big logs for the fireplaces, had once stopped to watch in amazement as she carried a tremendous iron caldron filled with hot water from the cookhouse to a nearby stream. He did not have to pay her old master, Doc Thompson, very much for her hire because she was a woman. If she could do a man's work, he'd be getting a bargain.

"We can try it," he said. "If it don't work out you'll have to go back to cooking and cleaning."

But it did work out. Harriet was delighted. She knew that Stewart was pleased with the new arrangement for shortly afterward he allowed her to "hire her time." This was a privilege which was extended to trustworthy slaves who were good workers. It meant that Harriet could find jobs for herself, and would pay Stewart fifty or sixty dollars a year. Whatever she earned over and beyond this sum, she was allowed to keep.

She sought and found jobs that would keep her out of doors. She hauled logs, plowed fields, drove an oxcart. She became a familiar figure in the fields—a slender, muscular young woman, with her skirts looped up around her waist and a vivid bandanna tied on her head.

During this period, she often worked with Ben, her father. John Stewart placed Ben in charge of the slaves who cut the timber which was to be sent by boat to the Baltimore shipyard. For weeks at a time Harriet swung a broadax in the woods, cutting half a cord of wood.

She learned most of the woods lore that she knew from Ben: the names of birds, which berries were good to eat and which were poisonous, where to look for water lilies, how to identify the hemlocks and the plant that he called cranebill, wild geranium or crane's bill.

Harriet was an apt pupil. Ben said that her eyes were sharper than his. She said, ''No. It's not just my eyes. It's my hands, too.'' She thought her hands seemed to locate the root or herb she was seeking before she actually saw it.

Ben taught her how to pick a path through the woods, even through the underbrush, without making a sound. He said, ''Any old body can go through a woods crashing and mashing things down like a cow. That's easy. You practice doing it the hard way—move so quiet even a bird on a nest don't hear you and fly up.''

When she was nineteen, Ben rewarded her efforts with praise. She had followed him through the woods and though he moved quietly himself, he had not heard her, although she was close behind. When they reached a clearing, she came up in back of him and touched him on the arm. He jumped, startled, and then laughed when he saw Harriet standing beside him.

She was tremendously pleased by this. She thought if only her master, John Stewart, would stop having her exhibit her strength for the entertainment of his guests, she would be content to spend the rest of her life on this plantation hiring herself out.

Unfortunately, Stewart had long since discovered that she was as strong as any of the men on the plantation. She could lift barrels of produce, could shoulder heavy timbers. Whenever he had visitors, he gave orders that she was to be hitched to a boat loaded with stone and was to drag it behind her as she walked along the edge of the river. She could hear cries of astonishment, laughter, applause from the men who stood on the bank watching. This audience of fashionably dressed planters made her feel that she was little better than a trained animal.

Though Stewart continued to have her perform for his friends, she remained with him, hiring her time, for six years.

9

The Patchwork Quilt

IN 1843, HARRIET ROSS began to make a patchwork quilt. She had trouble finding the brilliantly colored pieces of cotton cloth she needed. Sewing the quilt together was even harder.

The needle kept slipping through her fingers. Sometimes she did not know that she had lost it, until she tried to take a stitch and found that she held only a long piece of thread. It seemed as though she would never be able to master the art of sewing, to make the needle go through the material where she wanted it to go. It was the hardest task she had ever undertaken.

Yet as the quilt pattern developed, she thought it was as beautiful as the wild flowers that grew in the woods and along the edge of the roads. The yellow was like the Jerusalem flower, and the purple suggested motherwort, and the white pieces were like water lily, and the varying shades of green represented the leaves of all the plants.

For this was no ordinary quilt. It would be trousseau, and the entire contents of what under different circumstances would have been a hope chest. Harriet had fallen in love. She was going to marry a young man named John Tubman. He was a tall, well-built fellow, with a ready laugh, and a clear lilting whistle.

She thought about him while she sewed, how tall he was, how sweet the sound of his whistling. She was so short she had to look up to him. She looked up to him for another reason, too. He was free. He had always been free. Yet he wanted to marry her and she was a slave.

They were married in 1844. Harriet went to live in his cabin, taking with her her one beautiful possession, the patchwork quilt.

The knowledge that she was still a slave bothered her more and more. If she were sold, she would be separated from John. She truly loved him. She had asked him how he came to be free. He said it was because his mother and father had been freed by their master, at the time of the master's death.

This made Harriet wonder about her own family, especially Old Rit, who was forever talking about the promises of freedom that had been made to her. She paid five dollars to a lawyer to look up the wills of the various masters to whom Old Rit had belonged. It had taken her years to save five dollars, she had hoarded pennies to accumulate such a sum. But it seemed to her the information was well worth the cost. She found that Old Rit had originally been willed to a young woman named Mary Patterson, with the provision that she was to be freed when she was forty-five. Mary Patterson died shortly afterward, still unmarried. According to the lawyer, Old Rit should have been freed long ago.

After this, Harriet grew more and more discontented. She felt that she was a slave only because Old Rit had been tricked and deceived, years ago.

Times were hard the year that Harriet married John Tubman. And the next year, too. One of the house servants said the trouble was due in the price of cotton. Dr. Thompson had said so. He said cotton brought thirteen cents a pound in 1837, and when it was high, the slave traders paid as much as a thousand dollars for prime field hands. Then cotton started going down, until now in 1845 it was bringing only five cents a pound, and the slave traders gave less than five hundred dollars for young strong slaves.

Harriet decided that from the dilapidated look of the plantation—fields lying fallow, the Big House in need of repair—Doc Thompson would soon be selling slaves again. He wouldn't be able to get much for them in Maryland, so in spite of the old master's will, he would sell them South.

She told John Tubman this. Every time she said it, she spoke of going North, of running away, following the North Star.

He warned her against such foolishness. What would she find there that she didn't have here? She hired her time, and so she always had a little money of her own. They had a cabin to themselves. Maryland was a good place to live.

He said that if she went North, she'd freeze to death. Besides, what happened to the ones who went there? None of them came back to tell what it was like. Why was that? Because they couldn't. They died there. If they were still alive, they would have returned to show the way to some of the rest of the slaves. What would she have there that she didn't have here?

Her reply was always the same: "I'd be free."

She told him about the dreams she had, how night after night, she dreamed that men on horseback came riding into the quarter, and then she heard the shrieks and screams of women and children, as they were put into the chain gang, that the screaming of the women made her wake up. She would lie there in the dark of the cabin, sweating, and, though awake, she could still hear the echo of·screams.

When she went back to sleep she would dream again. This time she was flying. She flew over cotton fields and cornfields, and then she flew over Cambridge and the Choptank River, and she could see the gleam of the water, and then she came to a mountain and flew over that. At last she reached a barrier, sometimes a fence, sometimes a river, and she couldn't fly over it.

She said, ''It appeared like I wouldn't have the strength, and just as I was sinking down, there would be ladies all dressed in white and they would put out their arms and pull me across—''

John Tubman disliked these dreams. When she retold them, her husky voice pitched low, she made them sound as though they had really happened. He thought this showed how restless and impatient she had become. He laughed at her, finally. He said that she must be related to Old Cudjo, who was so slow-witted he never laughed at a funny story until a half hour after it was told. Because only a slow-witted person would have the same dream all the time.

In spite of his derision, she kept telling him about her dreams. She said that on clear nights the North Star seemed to beckon to her. She was sure she could follow that star. They could go North together. Then she would be free too.

He decided he would put an end to this talk of

escape, of the North, and freedom. He asked what she would do when the sky was dark. Then how would she know which way was North? She wouldn't know which way to go. He would not go with her. He was perfectly satisfied where he was. She would be alone, in the dark. What would she eat? Where would she get food?

She started to say: in the woods. She could live a long time on the edible berries and fruit that she had long ago learned to recognize. And yet—she had seen many a half-starved runaway brought back in chains, not enough flesh left on him to provide a decent meal for a buzzard. Perhaps she, too, would starve. She remembered the time she ran away from Miss Susan's and crawled into a pigpen, remembered fighting with the pigs, pushing them away, to get at the trough. After four days she had been indistinguishable from the pigs, filthy, foul-smelling—and starving. So she had gone back to Miss Susan. The memory of this experience made her avoid John's eyes.

Perhaps her silence made him angry. He may have interpreted it as evidence of her stubbornness, her willfulness, her utter disregard of all his warnings, and so made a threat which would put a stop to this crazy talk about freedom.

He shouted at her, ''You take off and I'll tell the Master. I'll tell the Master right quick.''

She stared at him, shocked, thinking, he couldn't, he wouldn't. If he told the master that she was missing, she would be caught before she got off the plantation. John knew what happened to runaways who were caught and brought back. Surely he would not betray his own wife.

And yet—she knew that there were slaves who had betrayed other slaves when they tried to escape. Sometimes they told because they were afraid of the master, it was always hard on the ones who were left behind. Sometimes the house servants were the betrayers, they were closest to the masters, known to be tattletales, certain to be rewarded because of their talebearing.

But John Tubman was free. And free blacks helped the runaways. It was one of the reasons the masters disliked and distrusted them. Surely John would not deny freedom to her, when he had it himself. Perhaps he was afraid he would be held responsible for her escape, afraid the master would think John had incited her to run away. Besides, he was satisfied here, he had said so.

Then she thought, frowning, but if a man really loved a woman, wouldn't he be willing to take risks to help her to safety? She shook her head. He must have been joking, or speaking through a sudden uncontrollable anger.

"You don't mean that," she said slowly. But he

did mean it. She could tell by the way he looked at her.

For the tall young man with the gay laugh, and the merry whistle, had been replaced by a hostile stranger, who glared at her as he said, ''You just start and see.''

She knew that no matter what words she might hear during the rest of her life, she would never again hear anything that hurt like this. It was as though he had deliberately tried to kill all the trust and love and devotion she had for him.

That night as she lay beside him on the floor of the cabin, she felt that he was watching her, waiting to see if this was the night when she would try to leave.

From that night on, she was afraid of him.

"A Glory over Everything"

ONE DAY, IN 1849, when Harriet was working in the fields, near the edge of the road, a white woman wearing a faded sunbonnet went past, driving a wagon. She stopped the wagon, and watched Harriet for a few minutes. Then she spoke to her, asked her what her name was, and how she had acquired the deep scar on her forehead.

Harriet told her the story of the blow she had received when she was a girl. After that, whenever the woman saw her in the fields, she stopped to talk to her. She told Harriet that she lived on a farm, near Bucktown. Then one day she said, not looking at Harriet, but looking instead at the overseer, far off at the edge of the fields, "If you ever need any help, Harriet, ever need any help, why you let me know."

That same year the young heir to the Brodas estate died. Harriet mentioned the fact of his

death to the white woman in the faded sunbonnet, the next time she saw her. She told her of the
panic-stricken talk in the quarter, told her that the
slaves were afraid that the master, Dr. Thompson,
would start selling them. She said that Doc
Thompson no longer permitted any of them to
hire their time. The woman nodded her head,
clucked to the horse, and drove off, murmuring,
"If you ever need any help—"

The slaves were right about Dr. Thompson's
intention. He began selling slaves almost immediately. Among the first ones sold were two of
Harriet Tubman's sisters. They went South with
the chain gang on a Saturday.

When Harriet heard of the sale of her sisters,
she knew that the time had finally come when
she must leave the plantation. She was reluctant
to attempt the long trip North alone, not because
of John Tubman's threat to betray her, but because she was afraid she might fall asleep some-
where along the way and so would be caught
immediately.

She persuaded three of her brothers to go with
her. Having made certain that John was asleep,
she left the cabin quietly, and met her brothers at
the edge of the plantation. They agreed that she
was to lead the way, for she was more familiar
with the woods than the others.

The three men followed her, crashing through the underbrush, frightening themselves, stopping constantly to say, ''What was that?'' or ''Someone's coming.''

She supposed they were doing the best they could but they moved very slowly. She kept getting so far ahead of them that she had to stop and wait for them to catch up with her, lest they lose their way. Their progress was slow, uncertain. Their feet got tangled in every vine. They tripped over fallen logs, and once one of them fell flat on his face. They jumped, startled, at the most ordinary sounds: the murmur of the wind in the branches of the trees, the twittering of a bird. They kept turning around, looking back.

They had not gone more than a mile when she became aware that they had stopped. She turned and went back to them. She could hear them whispering. One of them called out, ''Hat!''

''What's the matter? We haven't got time to keep stopping like this.''

''We're going back.''

''No,'' she said firmly. ''We've got a good start. If we move fast and move quiet—''

Then all three spoke at once. They said the same thing, over and over, in frantic hurried whispers, all talking at once:

They told her that they had changed their

minds. Running away was too dangerous. Someone would surely see them and recognize them. By morning the master would know they had "took off." Then the handbills advertising them would be posted all over Dorchester County. The patterollers would search for them. Even if they were lucky enough to elude the patrol, they could not possibly hide from the bloodhounds. The hounds would be baying after them, snuffing through the swamps and the underbrush, zigzagging through the deepest woods. The bloodhounds would surely find them. And everyone knew what happened to a runaway who was caught and brought back alive.

She argued with them. Didn't they know that if they went back they would be sold, if not tomorrow, then the next day, or the next? Sold South. They had seen the chain gangs. Was that what they wanted? Were they going to be slaves for the rest of their lives? Didn't freedom mean anything to them?

"You're afraid," she said, trying to shame them into action. "Go on back. I'm going North alone."

Instead of being ashamed, they became angry. They shouted at her, telling her that she was a fool and they would make her go back to the plantation with them. Suddendly they surrounded her, three men, her own brothers, jostling her, pushing her along, pinioning her; arms behind her. She fought against them, wasting her strength, exhausting herself in a furious struggle.

She was no match for three strong men. She said, panting, "All right. We'll go back. I'll go with you."

She led the way, moving slowly. Her thoughts were bitter. Not one of them was willing to take a small risk in order to be free. It had all seemed so perfect, no simple, to have her brothers go with her, sharing the dangers of the trip together, just as a family should. Now if she ever went North, she would have to go alone.

Two days later, a slave working beside Harriet in the fields motioned to her. She bent toward him, listening. He said the water boy had just brought news to the field hands, and it had been passed from one to the other until it reached him. The news was that Harriet and her brothers had been sold to the Georgia trader, and that they were to be sent South with the chain gang that very night.

Harriet went on working but she knew a moment of panic. She would have to go North alone. She would have to start as soon as it was dark. She could not go with the chain gang. She might die on the way, because of those inexplicable sleeping seizures. But then she—how could she run away? She might fall asleep in plain view along the road.

Afterward, she explained her decision to run the risk of going North alone, in these words: "I had reasoned this out in my mind; there was one of two things I had a *right* to, liberty or death; if I could not have one, I would have the other; for no man should take me alive; I should fight for my liberty as long as my strength lasted, and when the time came for me to go, the Lord would let them take me."

At dusk, when the work in the fields was over, she started toward the Big House. She had to let someone know that she was going North, someone she could trust. She no longer trusted John Tubman and it gave her a lost, lonesome feeling. Her sister Mary worked in the Big House, and she planned to tell Mary that she was going to run away, so someone would know.

As she went toward the house, she saw the master, Doc Thompson, riding up the drive on his horse. She turned aside and went toward the quarter. A field hand had no legitimate reason for entering the kitchen of the Big House—and yet— there must be some way she could leave word so that afterward someone would think about it and know that she had left a message.

As she went toward the quarter she began to

sing. Dr. Thompson reined in his horse, turned around and looked at her. It was not the beauty of her voice that made him turn and watch her, frowning, it was the words of the song that she was singing, and something defiant in her manner, that disturbed and puzzled him.

> When that old chariot comes,
>   I'm going to leave you,
> I'm bound for the promised land,
>   Friends, I'm going to leave you.
>
> I'm sorry, friends, to leave you,
>   Farewell! Oh, farewell!
> But I'll meet you in the morning,
>   Farewell! Oh, farewell!
>
> I'll meet you in the morning,
>   When I reach the promised land;
> On the other side of Jordan,
>   For I'm bound for the promised land.

That night when John Tubman was asleep, and the fire had died down in the cabin, she took the ashcake that had been baked for their breakfast, and a good-sized piece of salt herring, and tied them together in an old bandanna. By hoarding this small stock of food, she could make it last a long time, and with the berries and edible roots she could find in the woods, she wouldn't starve.

She decided that she would take the quilt with her, too. Her hands lingered over it. It felt soft and warm to her touch. Even in the dark, she thought she could tell one color from another, because she knew its pattern and design so well.

Once she was off the plantation, she took to the woods, not following the North Star, not even looking for it, going instead toward Bucktown. She needed help. She was going to ask the white woman who had stopped to talk to her so often if she would help her. Perhaps she wouldn't. But she would soon find out.

When she came to the farmhouse where the woman lived, she approached it cautiously, circling around it. It was so quiet. There was no sound at all, not even a dog barking, or the sound of voices. Nothing.

She tapped on the door, gently. A voice said, "Who's there?" She answered, "Harriet, from Dr. Thompson's place."

When the woman opened the door she did not seem at all surprised to see her. She glanced at the little bundle that Harriet was carrying, at the quilt, and invited her in. Then she sat down at the kitchen table, and wrote two names on a slip of paper, and handed the paper to Harriet.

She said that those were the next places where it was safe for Harriet to stop. The first place was a farm where there was a gate with big white posts and round knobs on top of them. The people there would feed her, and when they thought it was safe for her to go on, they would tell her how to get to the next house, or take her there. For these were the first two stops on the Underground Railroad—going North, from the Eastern Shore of Maryland.

Thus Harriet learned that the Underground Railroad that ran straight to the North was not a railroad at all. Neither did it run underground. It was composed of a loosely organized group of people who offered food and shelter, or a place of concealment, to fugitives who had set out on the long road to the North and freedom.

Harriet wanted to pay this woman who had befriended her. But she had no money. She gave her the patchwork quilt, the only beautiful object she had ever owned.

That night she made her way through the woods, crouching in the underbrush whenever she heard the sound of horses' hoofs, staying there until the riders passed. Each time she wondered if they were already hunting for her. It would be so easy to describe her, the deep scar on her forehead like a dent, the old scars on the back of her neck, the husky speaking voice, the lack of height, scarcely five feet tall. The master would say she was wearing rough clothes when she ran away, that she had a bandanna on her head, that she was muscular and strong.

She knew how accurately he would describe her. One of the slaves who could read used to tell the others what it said on those handbills that were nailed up on the trees, along the edge of the roads. It was easy to recognize the handbills that advertised runaways, because there was always a picture in one corner, a picture of a black man, a little running figure with a stick over his shoulder, and a bundle tied on the end of the stick.

In the morning, she came to the house where her friend had said she was to stop. She showed the slip of paper that she carried to the woman who answered her knock at the back door of the farmhouse. The woman fed her, and then handed her a broom and told her to sweep the yard.

Harriet hesitated, suddenly suspicious. Then she decided that with a broom in her hand, working in the yard, she would look as though she belonged on the place, certainly no one would suspect that she was a runaway.

That night the woman's husband, a farmer, loaded a wagon with produce. Harriet climbed in. He threw some blankets over her, and the wagon started.

It was dark under the blankets, and not exactly comfortable. But Harriet decided that riding was better than walking. She was surprised at her own lack of fear, wondered how it was that she so readily trusted these strangers who might betray her. For all she knew, the man driving the wagon might be taking her straight back to the master.

She thought of those other rides in wagons, when she was a child, the same clop-clop of the horses' feet, creak of the wagon, and the feeling of being lost because she did not know where she was going. She did not know her destination this time either, but she was not alarmed.

The next morning when the stars were still visible in the sky, the farmer stopped the wagon. Harriet was instantly awake.

He told her to follow the river, to keep following it to reach the next place where people would take her in and feed her. He said that she must travel only at night, and she must stay off the roads because the patrol would be hunting for her. Harriet climbed out of the wagon. "Thank you," she said simply, thinking how amazing it was that there should be white people who were willing to go to such lengths to help a slave get to the North.

When she finally arrived in Pennsylvania, she had traveled roughly ninety miles from Dorchester County. She had slept on the ground outdoors at night. She had been rowed for miles up the Choptank River by a man she had never seen before. She had been concealed in a haycock, and had, at one point, spent a week hidden in a potato hole in a cabin which belonged to a family of free blacks. She had been hidden in the attic of the home of a Quaker. She had been befriended by stout German farmers, whose guttural speech surprised her and whose well-kept farms astonished her. She had never before seen barns and fences, farmhouses and outbuildings, so carefully painted. The cattle and horses were so clean they looked as though they had been scrubbed.

When she crossed the line into the free state of Pennsylvania, the sun was coming up. She said, "I looked at my hands to see if I was the same person now I was free. There was such a glory over everything, the sun came like gold through the trees, and over the fields, and I felt like I was in heaven."

11

Stranger in a Strange Land

HARRIET TUBMAN'S moment of exultation passed quickly. According to her own words: "There was no one to welcome me to the land of freedom. I was a stranger in a strange land, and my home after all was down in the old cabin quarter with the old folks, and my brothers and sisters."

When she thought of her family, left behind in Maryland, all of them slaves, her joy in having escaped rapidly left her. She decided that as soon as she could, she would go back to Dorchester County and lead her family North, too. She knew the way now.

But she had done it once, alone, and with the help of the Lord, she would do it again, and again, until she got all of her family out of Maryland.

That year, 1849, she went to work in a hotel in Philadelphia, as a cook. She had always hated housework. She felt trapped inside the kitchen where she worked. Yet she stayed there a year, cooking, washing dishes and pots and pans, scrubbing the floor. She saved most of the money she earned, hoarding the tips she was given. She would need money when she went back into slave territory.

At first she found Philadelphia a strange and frightening place. The streets were filled with people. There was the constant movement of horses and wagons and fine carriages. The buildings were taller than any she had ever seen.

She knew moments of homesickness when she longed for the quarter, remembering the old familiar smoky smell of the cabin, the good smell of the earth when it was plowed in the spring.

Early in 1850 she visited the office of the Philadelphia Vigilance Committee. Sooner or later all fugitive slaves in the city went there seeking information about their relatives, or with requests for help of one kind or another. It was in this office, upstairs in Lebanon Seminary, that she learned the extent of the network of stops on the Underground Railroad. By 1850 the road was doing a tremendous volume of business. Philadelphia was its principal center in the East.

William Still, a black man, was the secretary of the Vigilance Committee. J. Miller McKim, a

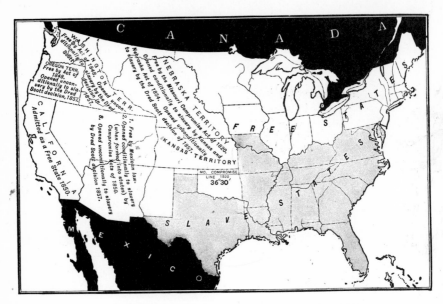

Areas of freedom and slavery in the mid-1850s.

Quaker, was the president. The Committee and its members were prepared to offer assistance to fugitives at any hour of the day or night; it might be in the form of food, clothing, money, railroad tickets, or a place to hide.

Again and again Harriet went back to the office of the Vigilance Committee. As she listened to the stories that Still told, she came to the conclusion that almost any slave who had the courage to run away was certain to reach his destination—the North. But the slaves did not know this. She decided that she would spread the word through Maryland. She herself, by accident, or intuition, or the grace of God, had come all the way from

Dorchester County on the Underground Railroad—and on her own two feet. As soon as she had saved money enough to take care of any emergencies that might arise, she would go back there for her family—and anyone else who wanted to be free.

In December, 1850, she arranged for the escape of her sister, her sister's husband, John Bowley, and their two children, one of them a baby. Though John Bowley was free, his wife and children were slaves. He had learned that his family was to be sold. When he received this information, he went to a Quaker friend of his for advice and help. This man was an agent of the Underground Railroad who lived in Cambridge, Maryland.

The Quaker agent in Cambridge, knowing, as all such people did, that he was watched constantly, and that his mail might be censored, sent a message to William Still in Philadelphia. The message, which was passed along the underground route, from one person to another, said that there were two large bales of wool and two small ones that would have to be transported from Baltimore to Philadelphia. The Cambridge agent said that a small boat would be available for the shipment from Cambridge to Baltimore but he was worried about the trip from there to Philadelphia.

In Philadelphia, almost every evening after work, Harriet climbed the long flight of stairs which led to a loft in the building which housed Lebanon Seminary. This served as the office for the Philadelphia Vigilance Committee. She was fascinated by the stories she heard told in that big bare room. Quite often a party of fugitive slaves arrived while she was there, and she watched William Still write their names in the big notebook that he kept, not only their names but something of their history, too.

On several occasions she had seen runaways who came from the Eastern Shore. Thus she was able to get a little thirdhand information about her father and mother, Ben and Old Rit, or about one of her brothers or sisters.

One night, a quiet night there, in the loft, William Still was talking to J. Miller McKim, and to Harriet, when a stranger entered the office. He nodded to Harriet and then went over to the desk where he carried on a low-voiced conversation with Still and McKim.

Suddenly Still beckoned to Harriet. ''Maybe you can help us find a woman to—'' Then he interrupted himself. ''There's a man named—'' Even though no outsider could have overheard him, he lowered his voice, ''Named John Bowley—''

"Bowley?" Harriet said. "John Bowley? Where's he from?"

"From Cambridge, Maryland. And—"

"Why that's my brother-in-law," she said, excitement in her voice. "He's married to my sister Mary—and—why he's a free man. What's the trouble?"

"Yes, he's free," said Still. "But his wife and children are slaves. And they are about to be sold. We know how to get them to Baltimore. But we've got to find someone to guide them from Baltimore to Philadelphia, preferably a woman, because there's a baby and another child. We thought you might know of a woman who would—"

"I will," she said promptly.

But Mr. Still shook his head. He said that it was difficult for free Negroes with all their papers in order to leave Baltimore. For her to attempt to bring them out when she was a fugitive herself would be an impossibility. They would be weighed, measured, at the railroad station or at the dock, and this information would be compared with the descriptions of all other known runaways. Even if this family bore no resemblance to any other fugitives, they still could not leave until they had obtained a bond signed by two well-known residents.

Harriet laughed. "Mr. Still, you're trying to

scare me. And I don't scare easy. Besides, I know enough about the Underground Railroad now so that I know you don't have to go through any weighing and measuring to get a group of people out of Baltimore. That's my sister and her husband and her children and I'm the one that's going to Baltimore to get them.''

William Still threw up his hands. ''All right,'' he said, ''but please, please, be careful.''

On the morning that a message arrived saying that all the necessary, careful arrangements had been completed, John Bowley's wife and two children had been already picked up with a group of slaves and placed in the slave pen at the Courthouse in Cambridge. The auction had started that morning with the sale of prime field hands. No one showed any interest in purchasing the women and children in the lot.

At noon the auctioneer called a recess. He said that he would put the females on the block later on in the day, and went off to the inn to get his dinner. He paused a moment in the doorway and grumbled to the guard, ''Much good it will do to put 'em up. Not much interest in 'em.''

Meanwhile John Bowley and his Quaker friend had evolved a plan, a bold and desperate plan, which might or might not work.

Shortly after the auctioneer went to the inn,

John entered the courthouse, carrying a large white official-looking envelope. He handed it to the guard who stood near the slave pen, and said, ''It's a message from my master, the auctioneer. He wants me to bring that woman and the two children over to the inn.'' He gestured toward his family. ''He thinks he's got a buyer for them.''

The guard opened the envelope, read the message, nodded his head. Then because John extended his hand, he handed the envelope and the note back to him. Opening the gate of the pen, he went inside, ''Get along there now,'' he said, pushing the woman and her two children out, separating them from the others.

John walked down the street beside them, still holding the envelope as though it were a talisman. They moved slowly. His wife was carrying the baby and the small child walked beside her, holding on to her skirts.

It was noon so there was no one on the street. The town seemed asleep in the cold sunlight. He supposed folks were all in their houses eating, even the children. He kept thinking that it ought to take the auctioneer about two hours to eat and drink and talk up the afternoon's sale. He crossed the street with his family, still moving slowly, breathing hard, appalled at his own daring. But it was either this—doing what he had done—or lose his wife and children, for good.

Halfway down the street, he paused, looked back. The street was empty. "Quick, now!" he said. He opened the gate of a picket fence in front of one of the big houses. "Hurry, hurry!" he said, urging them to go faster, around the side of the house, to the back door. As they approached the door it opened for them.

His Quaker friend said, "Thee made it, John, with the help of the Lord, as I knew thee would."

They stayed in the attic of the house until dark. Then they went downstairs to the kitchen where they were fed. After they finished eating, the Quaker led them out of the house. There was a farmer's wagon in the dooryard. They climbed in, lay on the floor of the wagon. Blankets were thrown over them.

It was not a long ride but it was a jouncy one. When the wagon stopped and the driver got down and threw the blankets back, John knew he was near the river, he could smell it.

All of them got in a rowboat at the edge of the river. The driver of the wagon rowed them out to a small fishing boat where John Bowley and his family embarked for Baltimore.

There was food on the boat and blankets, and he knew where he was going, knew how to sail a boat, knew that he would be met by someone, and yet he was vaguely uneasy. The children went to sleep quickly. He and his wife talked, not a lot, just now and then. If it weren't for the feeling of uncertainty, pinprick of fear, he would have enjoyed sailing up the Chesapeake on this cold starry night. He was sailing without lights, and so was more aware of the night than he had ever been. He could smell fish from the boat, could see lights from other boats.

He had been told that when he got near Baltimore, he was to watch for two lights, close together, a yellow one and a blue one, When he saw them he was to get in the dinghy and row to them. He kept worrying about it. Suppose he missed the lights, suppose—

Toward morning there was faint color in the sky, not really daylight, a lifting of the darkness. He kept peering at the shore. Suddenly he saw the lights, a yellow one and a blue one, and sailed toward them. He got his wife and children in the dinghy and rowed shoreward.

As he drew nearer he saw where the lights came from—two barn lanterns, the shades tinted, one blue and the other yellow. There was a wagon quite close to the shore in a wooded area, a bent-over figure on the seat. To his surprise he saw that it was a woman, a white woman, tremendously fat, who turned and watched him as he got out of the boat.

"Who are you?" she asked.

At first he could only whisper. For he did not

know what to expect. Then he said, "A friend with friends." That was the password he had been told to use.

"God bless you, you made it," she said. "I've been watching for two mornings straight."

Then she started moving quickly for so large a woman. The wagon held potatoes and onions, not many of them, but quite a few. She rearranged the load. John and his wife lay down in the back of the wagon with the small child, and the fat woman took the baby and held it in her arms, then wrapped it loosely under the shawl she wore over her coat.

John thought, She's so big nobody's know that the baby was there.

The woman said, "I got to cover you up," and threw blankets over them.

Again it was a long jouncy ride. When the wagon stopped they were in the yard of a stable, and it was broad daylight. They stayed inside the stable all that day. The fat woman said she'd be back for them that night, and she gave them a package of food. They ate quickly, hungrily. Then they just sat waiting for night.

When it was dark the woman came for them. They climbed in the wagon again. This time they only went a short distance. The fat woman helped them out of the wagon, guided them toward the back door of a brick house. She tapped lightly at the door. Someone opened it. They all went inside.

John looked at the short stocky figure standing in the middle of the big warm kitchen. It was a man, a stranger, and yet—he thought the face was familiar. Then his wife said, laughing, "Harriet! It's Harriet!"

"A friend with friends," she said and chuckled.

They stayed in the house in Baltimore for a week. After that Harriet, fearless, self-assured, guided them from one station stop to the next. At each house, word was sent on to the next stop to be on the alert, to watch for this party of fugitives. Thus Harriet became aware of a new undercurrent of fear all along the route.

When she reached Philadelphia with her passengers, she took them straight to the office of the Philadelphia Vigilance Committee. There the talk was about the new Fugitive Slave Law, now three months old, and what it would mean to people like herself and to the people who offered them shelter. People convicted of harboring slaves could be imprisoned or fined so heavily that they would lose everything they owned. As for the runaways, they might be shot out of hand, or whipped and sold to the deep South, where they would die anyway. It was this that had created the undercurrent of fear.

12

Freedom's Clothes

LIKE OTHER RUNAWAY SLAVES, Harriet Tubman was no longer safe in Philadelphia. Because of the Fugitive Slave Law she was liable to be arrested at any moment even though she was living in a free state. It was now doubly dangerous for her to return to slave territory, yet in the spring of 1851 she went back to Dorchester County. She brought away one of her brothers and two other men, and got them safely through to Philadelphia.

That summer she worked in Cape May, New Jersey, in a hotel. She saved practically all of her earnings, living like a miser, hoarding each penny. She planned to go back to Maryland in the fall and she would need money to finance the trip.

This was to be a special trip with only one purpose behind it: to persuade John Tubman to go North with her. It had been two years since she had seen him. During that time she had not only forgiven him for his threat to betray her, but she had begun to remember all the things about him that had made her fall in love with him.

And so one night, in the fall of 1851, she arrived at the plantation again. She lingered in the woods, on the edge of the fields, impatiently anticipating the moment when she would see John face to face.

She was wearing a man's suit, a man's felt hat on her head. She felt perfectly safe, confident. She knew that the master, Dr. Thompson, would not expect her to return to the plantation from which she had once managed to escape. Besides, she had been back here before.

Late that night she went toward the cabin where she had lived with John Tubman, knocked softly. She heard the murmur of voices. Then John opened the door. At first she saw only his face, the familiar beloved face that she had for weeks now longed to see again. She had forgotten how tall he was—how broad his shoulders.

For the first time she noticed that he was not alone in the cabin. A woman got up from a stool near the fireplace, and came and stood beside him. She was young, slender, infinitely more attractive than Harriet.

Harriet tried to explain why she had come back but the words did not come easily. She felt like an outsider, a stranger. She was terribly aware of the man's suit, the burrs clinging to it, the material old and worn and snagged by briars, the man's shoes on her feet, the battered old hat. These two people standing there, side by side, silhouetted in the doorway, light from the fireplace behind them, seemed to belong in the cabin. Something in their posture suggested that she did not, that she was an intruder.

She spoke of the North, and how they could live there together, and possibly have children. There was a yearning tenderness in her voice. She said, "I came back for you, John."

"Me?" he said, and put his arm around the young woman. "This is Caroline," he said. "Caroline is my wife now. I'm not going North or anywhere else. I wouldn't leave here for nothing in the world." Then he laughed.

Harriet had wanted to hear him laugh again, hear that happy carefree laughter of his. But not this way. She hated the sound of it. It was mocking laughter, and the woman standing there beside him was laughing, too.

How wrong she had been to make plans for him. Why had she assumed that he would be willing to go North with her when he had refused before? She had forgotten that she had always been imbued with the idea of freedom, magic in the very sound of the word, and he had always been indifferent to it, perhaps because he possessed it himself. She thought with something like contempt he should have been a slave—he deserves to be one. She compared him with John Bowley, her brother-in-law, who was willing to risk his own life and safety, though he was a free man, in order that his wife and children should not be slaves.

She remembered how she had dreamed of living in Philadelphia with John Tubman. She wanted to plead with him. Then she knew a moment of anger and wanted to shout at them because she felt they had cheated her out of her dream, defrauded her. She hated this young woman who was now leaning against John, the look of puzzlement now replaced by disdain.

And yet—"I came back for you, John," she said again.

John and the woman laughed. Harriet stood there for a moment, wanting to cry. She thought of the long way she had come, of the money she had earned doing the housework that she hated, remembered how for months she had condemned him in her mind as worthless, and how that judgment had been softened by time, until she had remembered only the good in him, reexperiencing in retrospect the moments of warmth, of understanding, remembering how she had made the colorful quilt, dreaming about him like any young engaged girl. When she made the quilt, she was transformed. The field hand felling trees, cutting half a cord of wood a day, lifting barrels of flour, pulling loaded boats along the edge of the river like a horse, had been turned into a girl in love, melting with tenderness.

Even now she found it impossible to hate him. She was too much in love with him. But there was an emptiness, vast, unfillable, inside of her. It would stay with her forever.

Suddenly she remembered his previous threat. It wasn't safe to stay here. He might betray her. He had always said that he would.

She turned away, taking with her the memory of John Tubman and the young woman, Caroline, who had replaced her in his life.

By midnight she had collected a small group of slaves, all of whom wanted to be free, and started North with them, heading for Philadelphia.

The Legend of Moses

Up until the time of Harriet's discovery of John Tubman's infidelity, she had been guiding escaping slaves to the North and freedom largely because she wanted to rescue members of her own family. It is true that in each group she had conducted there were people who were not related to her, but the motive that had inspired the trips was always the same: to guide her own relatives into the free state of Pennsylvania.

After she discovered that John had found happiness with another woman, she brought a group of slaves North with her, none of whom was related to her.

During the next few months, she developed a much broader purpose. She pondered over the shocking contrast between the life of a field hand in Dorchester County, Maryland, and the life she had known and enjoyed in Philadelphia and in Cape May, New Jersey. The work she had done in

hotels was play compared to the terrible labors
she had performed as a slave. She was free to
change jobs for any reason—or for no reason at
all. She could go anywhere in Philadelphia, without a pass, and no one would question her. The
money that she earned was hers—all of it, to
spend as she pleased or to save. To a woman who
had been a slave, these were some of the great,
incredible wonders of freedom. She felt that all
men should enjoy these same rights and priv-
ileges.

Like the Abolitionists, she believed slavery to
be morally wrong—for masters and slaves alike.
She knew that she could not hope to end this evil
by herself but she thought she might help make
the ownership of slaves unprofitable in the area
she knew so well, the Eastern Shore of Maryland.
She was certain that even timid, frightened slaves
would run away if someone they could trust offered to guide them to the North. She decided to
keep going back to "the land of Egypt" as she
called Maryland, bringing more and more away.
She would leave directions for the bold, self-
assured ones, drawing maps for them on the dirt
floor of the cabins, carefully describing the stopping places on the route, so that they could make
the trip North without a conductor. Thus she
could slowly, steadily, increase the number of
runaways from that one area.

Up until 1851, she was either unaware of the danger posed by the Fugitive Slave Law, or else she ignored it. But that year the significance of the new law was brought home to her, in terms of people. In Philadelphia, she heard stories about three different runaways who had run afoul of the law, for these stories were being told everywhere—North and South.

The first alarming story she heard was about a runaway named Shadrach. He was arrested in Boston, on February 15, 1851, charged with being a fugitive slave. He was taken before a Federal Commissioner in the United States Courtroom for a hearing. A great crowd collected to hear the case, for this was the first test of the new law in Boston. The hearing had barely started when the Commissioner adjourned the court, to the great surprise of the people who were present.

The crowd began to leave the courtroom, moving slowly. Suddenly a group of black men came into the room, walked over to Shadrach, and surrounded him. One of them said to him, "Follow me." Shadrach, the runaway slave, was outside the courthouse before the police officers, who were guarding him, were aware that they had just watched an impromptu and wonderfully effective rescue party at work.

Shadrach was hidden in Boston. When the search for him had ended, the Boston Vigilance

Committee sent him on to Canada via the Underground Railroad.

Harriet was upset by this story, in spite of its happy ending. She had always thought of Boston as a safe place, a haven, for runaway slaves, just like Philadelphia.

Then in April, of that same year, she heard talk about a boy named Thomas Sims. He was walking along a street in Boston on the night of April 3, 1851, when he was arrested. George Ticknor Curtis, the United States Commissioner, who presided at the hearing, decided that Sims, who was a fugitive slave, must be returned to his owner in Georgia. The pro-slavery crowd in the courtroom cheered, pleased with the decision. But the Abolitionists were appalled, and talked of rescuing Sims.

But rescue was impossible. The courthouse was surrounded by a heavy chain and patrolled by a strong police force.

Sims was the first slave to be sent back into slavery by Massachusetts since the Revolution. He reached Savannah, Georgia, on the 19th, aboard the brig *Acorn*, which was owned in Boston, and had been chartered by the United States Government for the express purpose of returning the fugitive to his master.

Harriet kept hearing about Thomas Sims: That when he reached Savannah he was publicly whipped and then imprisoned for two months. After that he was sold and resold, first in Savannah, then in Charleston, then in New Orleans. He was finally taken to Vicksburg.

At first Harriet could not believe it possible that anyone could be taken out of the free state of Massachusetts and sent back to a slave state. The more she thought about it, the more it disturbed her.

The third story that Harriet Tubman heard about in Philadelphia that year concerned the slave Jerry, who was arrested in Syracuse, New York, on October 1, 1851. On that same day the Liberty Party was holding a convention in Syracuse. The delegates, having attended the morning session of the convention, had adjourned for dinner. While they were eating, they heard the slow tolling of the big bell on a nearby Congregational church.

Syracuse was an Abolitionist stronghold, and the church bells were used to give the alarm whenever a fugitive was in danger. The news spread quickly that Jerry had been arrested and was being held in the courthouse for a hearing. The streets were soon filled with men, women, children, dogs, all excited, all heading for the place where Jerry was held.

That night a group of men battered down the door of the courthouse, using a twenty-foot log.

Men armed with axes and crowbars forced their way to the second floor. The Marshal fired at them, and then jumped out of a window, his arm broken. The deputies left just as hastily. Jerry was taken out of his cell by his rescuers and finally sent to Canada and freedom, via the Underground Railroad.

Harriet Tubman heard the stories about the rescue of Shadrach, and of Jerry, about the return of Thomas Sims to Georgia, talked about, told and retold. These stories showed her exactly what the new law meant to runaway slaves living anywhere in the United States, and that, of course, included her. Yet she decided that she would not permit this new and stringent law to interfere with her plan to keep guiding slaves out of Dorchester County. It was now a well-known way. She recognized every creek and cove and inlet, every neck of land, every hiding place, every curve in the roads, every potential source of danger, every potential source of safety. She knew the people who lived in the farmhouses, knew which ones would welcome her and offer food and a night's lodging, knew which ones would set after her with guns and hounds.

But the next trip she made could not end in Philadelphia. Her passengers, as she called the fugitives who would travel with her, would not be safe there, would not be safe in Boston or in

"At first she had been called Minta or Minty. After her defiance of the overseer, they called her Harriet. Now they called her Moses."

Syracuse—or anywhere else in the United States. She would have to take them all the way to Canada. It would be a long trip, longer than any she had ever made, through territory that was strange and new to her, with the known hazard of the Fugitive Slave Law pacing her every footstep.

Though she was not aware of it, she had become a legend in the slave cabins along the Eastern Shore. She had always had the makings of a legend in her: the prodigious strength, the fearlessness, the religious ardor, the visions she had in which she experienced moments of prescience.

The slaves said she could see in the dark like a mule, that she could smell danger down the wind like a fox, that she could move through thick underbrush without making a sound, like a field mouse.

They said, voices muted, awed, that she talked with God every day, just like Moses. They said there was some strange power in her so that no one could die when she was with them. She enveloped the sick and the dying with her strength, sending it from her body to theirs, sustaining them.

They changed her name again. At first she had been called Minta or Minty. After her defiance of the overseer, they called her Harriet.

Now they called her Moses.

The Railroad Runs to Canada

ALONG THE EASTERN SHORE of Maryland, in Dorchester County, in Caroline County, the masters kept hearing whispers about the man named Moses, who was running off slaves. At first they did not believe in his existence. The stories about him were fantastic, unbelievable. Yet they watched for him. They offered rewards for his capture.

They never saw him. Now and then they heard whispered rumors to the effect that he was in the neighborhood. The woods were searched. The roads were watched. There was never anything to indicate his whereabouts. But a few days afterward, a goodly number of slaves would be gone from the plantation.

Unfortunately, the discovery was almost always made on a Sunday. Thus a whole day was lost before the machinery of pursuit could be set in motion. The posters offering rewards for the fugitives could not be printed until Monday. The men who made a living hunting for runaway slaves were out of reach, off in the woods with their dogs and their guns, in pursuit of four-footed game, or they were in camp meetings saying their prayers with their wives and families beside them.

In December, 1851, when she started out with the band of fugitives that she planned to take to Canada, she had been in the vicinity of the plantation for days, planning the trip, carefully selecting the slaves that she would take with her.

There were eleven in this party, including one of her brothers and his wife. It was the largest group that she had ever conducted, but she was determined that more and more slaves should know what freedom was like.

She had to take them all the way to Canada. The Fugitive Slave Law was no longer a great many incomprehensible words written down on the country's lawbooks. The new law had become a reality. It was Thomas Sims, a boy, picked up on the streets of Boston at night and shipped back to Georgia. It was Jerry and Shadrach, arrested and jailed with no warning.

She had never been in Canada. The route beyond Philadelphia was strange to her. But she could not let the runaways who accompanied her know this. As they walked along she told them stories of her own first flight, she kept painting vivid word pictures of what it would be like to be free.

They tried to sleep during the day but they never could wholly relax into sleep. She could tell by the positions they assumed, by their restless movements. And they walked at night. Their progress was slow. It took them three nights of walking to reach the first stop. She had told them about the place where they would stay, promising warmth and good food, holding these things out to them as an incentive to keep going.

When she knocked on the door of a farmhouse, a place where she and her parties of runaways had always been welcome, always been given shelter and plenty to eat, there was no answer. She knocked again, softly. A voice from within said, "Who is it?" There was fear in the voice.

She knew instantly from the sound of the voice that there was something wrong. She said, "A friend with friends," the password on the Underground Railroad.

The door opened, slowly. The man who stood in the doorway looked at her coldly, looked with unconcealed astonishment and fear at the eleven disheveled runaways who were standing near her. Then he shouted, ''Too many, too many. It's not safe. My place was searched last week. It's not safe!'' and slammed the door in her face.

She turned away from the house, frowning. She had promised her passengers food and rest and warmth, and instead of that, there would be hunger and cold and more walking over the frozen ground. Somehow she would have to instill courage into these eleven people, most of them strangers, would have to feed them on hope and bright dreams of freedom instead of the fried pork and corn bread and milk she had promised them.

She kept thinking, eleven of them. Eleven thousand dollars' worth of slaves. And she had to take them all the way to Canada. Sometimes she told them about Thomas Garrett, in Wilmington. She said he was their friend even though he did not know them. He was a Quaker and his speech was a little different from that of other people. His clothing was different, too. He wore the wide-brimmed hat that the Quakers wear.

She said that he had thick white hair, soft, almost like a baby's, and the kindest eyes she had ever seen. He was a big man and strong, but he had never used his strength to harm anyone, always to help people. He would give all of them a new pair of shoes. Everybody. He always did. Once they reached his house in Wilmington, they would be safe. He would see to it that they were.

She described the house where he lived, told them about the store where he sold shoes. She said he kept a pail of milk and a loaf of bread in the drawer of his desk so that he would have food ready at hand for any of God's poor who should suddenly appear before him, fainting with hunger. There was a hidden room in the store. A whole wall swung open, and behind it was a room where he could hide fugitives. On the wall there were shelves filled with small boxes—boxes of shoes—so that you would never guess that the wall actually opened.

While she talked, she kept watching them. They did not believe her. She could tell by their expressions. They were thinking, New shoes, Thomas Garrett, Quaker, Wilmington—what foolishness was this? Who knew if she told the truth? Where was she taking them anyway?

That night they reached the next stop—a farm that belonged to a German. She made the runaways take shelter behind trees at the edge of the fields before she knocked at the door. She hesitated before she approached the door, thinking, suppose that he, too, should refuse shelter, suppose—Then she thought, Lord, I'm going to hold steady on to You and You've got to see me through—and knocked softly.

She heard the familiar guttural voice say, "Who's there?"

She answered quickly, "A friend with friends."

He opened the door and greeted her warmly. "How many this time?" he asked.

"Eleven," she said and waited, doubting, wondering.

He said, "Good. Bring them in."

He and his wife fed them in the lamplit kitchen, their faces glowing, as they offered food and more food, urging them to eat, saying there was plenty for everybody, have more milk, have more bread, have more meat.

They spent the night in the warm kitchen. They really slept, all that night and until dusk the next day. When they left, it was with reluctance. They had all been warm and safe and well-fed. It was hard to exchange the security offered by that clean warm kitchen for the darkness and the cold of a December night.

15

"Go On or Die"

HARRIET HAD FOUND it hard to leave the warmth and friendliness, too. But she urged them on. For a while, as they walked, they seemed to carry in them a measure of contentment; some of the serenity and the cleanliness of that big warm kitchen lingered on inside them. But as they walked farther and farther away from the warmth and the light, the cold and the darkness entered into them. They fell silent, sullen, suspicious. She waited for the moment when some one of them would turn mutinous. It did not happen that night.

Two nights later she was aware that the feet behind her were moving slower and slower. She heard the irritability in their voices, knew that soon someone would refuse to go on.

She started talking about William Still and the Philadelphia Vigilance Committee. No one commented. No one asked any questions.

She told them about Frederick Douglass, the most famous of the escaped slaves, of his eloquence, of his magnificent appearance.

But they had been tired too long, hungry too long, afraid too long, footsore too long. One of them suddenly cried out in despair, "Let me go back. It is better to be a slave than to suffer like this in order to be free."

She carried a gun with her on these trips. She had never used it—except as a threat.

She lifted the gun, aimed it at the despairing slave. She said, "Go on with us or die." The husky low-pitched voice was grim.

He hesitated for a moment and then he joined the others. They started walking again. She tried to explain to them why none of them could go back to the plantation. If a runaway returned, he would turn traitor, the master and the overseer would force him to turn traitor. The returned slave would disclose the stopping places, the hiding places, the cornstacks they had used with the full knowledge of the owner of the farm.

She said, "We got to go free or die. And freedom's not bought with dust."

This time she told them about the long agony of the Middle Passage on the old slave ships, about the black horror of the holds, about the chains and the whips. They too knew these stories. But she wanted to remind them of the long hard way they had come, about the long hard way they had yet to go.

Thus she forced them to go on. Sometimes she thought she had become nothing but a voice speaking in the darkness, cajoling, urging, threatening. Sometimes she told them things to make them laugh, sometimes she sang to them, and heard the eleven voices behind her blending softly with hers, and then she knew that for the moment all was well with them.

She gave the impression of being a short, muscular, indomitable woman who could never be defeated. Yet at any moment she was liable to be seized by one of those curious fits of sleep, which might last for a few minutes or for hours.

Finally, they reached Thomas Garrett's house in Wilmington, Delaware. Just as Harriet had promised, Garrett gave them all new shoes, and provided carriages to take them on to the next stop.

By slow stages they reached Philadelphia, where William Still hastily recorded their names, and the plantations whence they had come, and something of the life they had led in slavery. Then he carefully hid what he had written, for fear it might be discovered. In 1872 he published this record in book form and called it *The Underground*

Railroad. In the foreword to his book he said: "While I knew the danger of keeping strict records, and while I did not then dream that in my day slavery would be blotted out, or that the time would come when I could publish these records, it used to afford me great satisfaction to take them down, fresh from the lips of fugitives on the way to freedom, and to preserve them as they had given them."

William Still, who was familiar with all the station stops on the Underground Railroad, supplied Harriet with money and sent her and her eleven fugitives on to Burlington, New Jersey.

Harriet felt safer now, though there were danger spots ahead. But the biggest part of her job was over. As they went farther and farther north, it grew colder; she was aware of the wind on the Jersey ferry and aware of the cold damp in New York. From New York they went on to Syracuse, where the temperature was even lower.

In Syracuse she met the Reverend J. W. Loguen, known as "Jarm" Loguen. This was the beginning of a lifelong friendship.

From Syracuse they went north again, into a colder, snowier city—Rochester. Here they almost certainly stayed with Frederick Douglass, for he wrote in his autobiography:

"On one occasion I had eleven fugitives at the same time under my roof, and it was necessary for them to remain with me until I could collect sufficient money to get them to Canada. It was the largest number I ever had at any one time, and I had some difficulty in providing so many with food and shelter, but, as may well be imagined, they were not very fastidious in either direction, and were well content with very plain food, and a strip of carpet on the floor for a bed, or a place on the straw in the barnloft.''

Late in December, 1851, Harriet arrived in St. Catharines, Canada West (now Ontario), with the eleven fugitives. It had taken almost a month to complete this journey; most of the time had been spent getting out of Maryland.

That first winter in St. Catharines was a terrible one. Harriet rented a small frame house in the town and set to work to make a home. The fugitives boarded with her. They worked in the forests, felling trees, and so did she. Sometimes she took other jobs, cooking or cleaning house for people in the town. She cheered on these newly arrived fugitives, working herself, finding work for them, finding food for them, praying for them, sometimes begging for them.

In spite of the severe cold, the hard work, she came to love St. Catharines, and the other towns and cities in Canada where black men lived. She discovered that freedom meant more than the right to change jobs at will, more than the right to keep the money that one earned. It was the right to vote and to sit on juries. It was the right to be elected to office. In Canada there were black men who were county officials and members of school boards. St. Catharines had a large colony of ex-slaves, and they owned their own homes, kept them neat and clean and in good repair. They lived in whatever part of town they chose and sent their children to the schools.

When spring came she decided that she would make this small Canadian city her home—as much as any place could be said to be home to a woman who traveled from Canada to the Eastern Shore of Maryland as often as she did.

In the spring of 1852, she went back to Cape May, New Jersey. She spent the summer there, cooking in a hotel. That fall she returned, as usual, to Dorchester County, and brought out nine more slaves.

She continued to live in this fashion, spending the winter in Canada, and the spring and summer working in Cape May, New Jersey, or in Philadelphia. She made two trips a year into slave territory, one in the fall and another in the spring. She now had a definite purpose, and her life fell into a pattern which remained unchanged for the next six years.

16

"Be Ready to Step on Board"

IN THE FALL OF 1854, Harriet Tubman began to feel uneasy about three of her brothers. Benjamin, John and William Henry were still in Maryland, working on plantations where they had been hired out.

It would not be safe to communicate with them directly. She could not read or write. So she had a friend write a cryptic letter to Jacob Jackson, who lived near the plantation where two of her brothers worked.

Jacob had an adopted son who had gone North to live. Harriet thought that it would be perfectly natural and understandable if this son should write to his foster father, reporting about his health and inquiring about the family. She either did not know or had forgotten that the son, William Henry, had no brothers and no "old folks."

When the letter arrived in Bucktown, the

postmaster opened it and read it. There was always the possibility that mail with a Northern postmark might contain Abolitionist propaganda, and when it was addressed to a free Negro, it was almost certain to contain objectionable material.

This is what he found: "Read my letter to the old folks, and give my love to them, and tell my brothers to be always *watching unto prayer, and when the good old ship of Zion comes along, to be ready to step on board.*" Signed—William Henry Jackson.

The postmaster showed the letter to two other men. They sent for Jacob, showed him the letter, and asked him for an explanation.

Jacob read the letter quickly, though he pretended to read it slowly, stumbling over the words, repeating some of them.

He handed the paper with its seemingly meaningless words back to the postmaster. "That letter can't be meant for me nohow," he said, shaking his head. "I can't make head or tail of it."

That same night, Jacob told all three of the Ross brothers that Moses would be coming for them soon, and to be ready to leave. Benjamin and John worked for Eliza Ann Brodins in Bucktown, William Henry worked on a plantation farther away. They said they would be ready when she came. John said he would be ready, too, but he looked worried.

Harriet made her way South, slowly, without incident. She reached Bucktown on the 23rd of December. The next night she started North again, with a larger party than she had planned for, though John Ross was not with them. Benjamin and William Henry were there. William Henry had brought his fiancée with him, Catherine (or Jane) Kane, a pretty girl, who had been a house servant. She was dressed in a boy's suit, and she looked like an attractive young boy. Then there were two strangers from Cambridge, Peter Jackson and John Chase.

When they were ready to start, John Ross, the third brother, had not arrived. Harriet started without him. She never waited for anyone. Delays were dangerous. She left word with Jacob for him, so that if he did come, he could overtake them along the way. The first stop would be in Caroline County, near Ben's cabin. Old Rit and Ben were now living forty miles to the north of Bucktown, in another county, but on a farm that belonged to Dr. Thompson.

John Ross did overtake them, finally. It was daybreak of Christmas morning when he found them. They were concealed in the fodder house, not far away from the cabin where Old Rit and Ben now lived.

John told them why he was late. His wife had

just had another baby. He had to go get the midwife. Then after the baby was born, he couldn't bear to leave her.

So he had lingered in the cabin, looking down at his wife and the newborn baby. Then he had edged toward the door, and each time he moved, his wife had said, ''Where you goin', John?''

Finally he had told her that he was leaving. He said that he would send Moses back for her, on her next trip. He had promised. It wouldn't be long—and in the dim light in the fodder house he looked at Moses for approval, for agreement. She nodded her head. So he felt better.

Then the girl, Catherine, saw John staring at her. She explained, with a toss of her head, that she was wearing a boy's suit because William Henry had bought it for her. It was the only way she had managed to get away so quickly, and with no trouble.

William Henry had been waiting for her, just off the plantation, on the road. He brought her right along with him. They'd be married when they got to the North—and freedom.

17

"Moses Arrives with Six Passengers"

It was still raining. From the dark, heavy look of the sky, visible through the roof of the fodder house, it would be an all-day rain. Christmas Day. And a Sunday. The beat of the rain against the roof of the fodder house, against its sides, would be their only Christmas greeting. She hoped they wouldn't resent it too much.

There were wide chinks in the walls. Through them she could see the sway-backed cabin where Daddy Ben and Old Rit lived. It looked exactly like the cabin on the Brodas plantation where she was born. A whole row of these sway-backed cabins here, too. Smoke kept pouring out of the clay-daubed chimney, hanging heavy in the air. Old Rit had probably killed her pig, and was cooking it for the Christmas dinner. The boys said that Old Rit was expecting them for dinner. They always spent Christmas Day with her.

She had to figure out some way of letting Ben know that she was here, that the boys were with her and that they needed food. It would never do to let Old Rit know this. She would laugh and shout.

Harriet remembered the two men, John Chase and Peter Jackson. They were strangers. She asked them to go to the cabin, to tell Ben that his children were in the fodder house, badly in need of food.

John and Peter did exactly as she told them. She watched them knock on the door of the cabin, saw Old Ben standing in the doorway. The men motioned to him to come outside. They talked to him. Ben nodded his head.

Late in the afternoon, he tapped on the side of the fodder house, and then opened the door, and put part of the Christmas dinner inside on the floor. He did not look at them. He said, ''I know what'll come of this and I ain't goin' *to see my children*, nohow.''

Harriet remembered his reputation for truthfulness. His word had always been accepted on the plantation because he was never known to tell a lie. She felt a kind of wondering admiration for him. How badly he must have wanted to see them; but he would not lie, and so he would not look at them. Thus, if he was questioned, he could say that he had not seen them.

"She had always had the makings of a legend in her: the prodigious strength, the fearlessness, the religious ardor, the visions. . . ."

He made three trips from the cabin to the fodder house. Each time he put a small bundle of food inside the door until he must have given them most of the food intended for the Christmas dinner. Harriet noticed how slow his movements were. He was stooped over. He had aged fast. She would have to come back soon for him and Old Rit. Some time very soon.

They stayed in the fodder house all that day, lying on top of the corn, listening to the drip of the rain, waiting for dark, when they would set out. They spoke in whispers.

Harriet kept reassuring them. They were perfectly safe. They would not be missed for at least two days. At Christmas everyone was busy, dancing, laughing.

She knew they did not like this long rainy day spent inside a fodder house, rain coming through the chinks in the boards. Dainty, pretty Catherine, who had been a house servant, complained bitterly.

Harriet laughed at her, and told her this was easy, just sitting around like this, that the Underground Railroad wasn't any train ride. It meant walking, and sometimes running, and being hungry, and sometimes jouncing up and down in the bottom of a farmer's wagon, but more walking than riding, rain or dry, through woods and swamps and briars and hiding anywhere that the earth offered a little shelter against prying eyes and listening ears.

Catherine let out a scream and then burst into tears and William Henry put his arm around her to comfort her. Harriet could not look at them. She turned her back on them, thinking not for her, ever, that soft light in a man's eyes.

Late in the afternoon, Ben made one more trip. He pushed another bundle of food inside the door. He kept his eyes closed, tight shut. He said he would be back when it got dark and would walk with them just a little way, to visit with them.

At dusk Harriet left the fodder house. She moved quietly toward the cabin. She wanted to get a good look at her mother.

When night came, Ben tapped at the door. He had tied a bandanna tight around his eyes. Harriet took one of his arms and one of the boys took him by the other arm. They started out, walking slowly.

Harriet answered Ben's questions as fast as she could, she told him a little about the other trips she had made, said that she would be back again to get him and Old Rit.

The next day, Monday, the brothers should have been back on the plantations where they worked. By afternoon, their temporary masters, disturbed by their absence, sent messengers to Dr. Thompson, in Caroline County, asking about them. Dr. Thompson said, ''Why, they generally come to see the house servants when they come

home for Christmas, but this time they haven't
been round at all. Better go down to Old Ben's
and ask him.''

They questioned Old Rit first. She said, ''Not
one of 'em came this Christmas. I was looking for
'em all day, and my heart's most broke about 'em
not coming.''

Ben said, ''I haven't *seen* one of 'em this
Christmas.''

Meanwhile Harriet led her group through the
woods. Sometimes she ventured on the road and
they stumbled along behind her over the frozen
ruts. She told them about Thomas Garrett, and
the food and the warmth of the welcome that
awaited them in Wilmington, and thought of the
many different times she had invoked the image
of the tall, powerfully built Quaker with the kind
eyes, to reassure a group of runaways who stumbled along behind her.

They stopped at a house in Middletown and
spent the night and part of the day. Then they
continued their journey, on through New Castle,
until they reached the Christiana River. Across
the river lay Wilmington.

Harriet waited until it was dark and then she
herded her party along, over the bridge, and then
straight toward Thomas Garrett's house. Garrett
fed them and hastily sent them on their way to

Philadelphia that same night. The next day Garrett wrote a letter to J. Miller McKim, to let him know that this party of fugitives was on its way:

Wilmington, 12 mo. 29th, 1854

Esteemed Friend, J. Miller McKim:—We made arrangements last night, and sent away Harriet Tubman, with six men and one woman to Allen Agnew's, to be forwarded across the country to the city. Harriet, and one of the men, had worn their shoes off their feet, and I gave them two dollars to help fit them out, and directed a carriage to be hired at my expense, to take them out, but do not yet know the expense. I now have two more from the lowest county in Maryland, on the Peninsula, upwards of one hundred miles. I will try to get one of our trusty colored men to take them tomorrow morning to the Anti-Slavery office. You can pass them on.

THOMAS GARRETT

They arrived safely at the office of the Philadelphia Vigilance Committee on the 29th of December, late at night. William Still wrote their names down in his record book under the heading "Moses Arrives With Six Passengers." He described Harriet as "a woman of no pretensions, indeed, a more ordinary specimen of humanity could hardly be found among the most unfortunate-looking farm hands of the South. . . .

"Her success was wonderful. Time and again she made successful visits to Maryland on the

Underground Rail Road, and would be absent for weeks at a time, running daily risks while making preparations for herself and passengers. Great fears were entertained for her safety, but she seemed wholly devoid of personal fear. The idea of being captured by slave-hunters or slave-holders, seemed never to enter her mind.''

He mentioned the sleeping seizures. ''Half of her time, she had the appearance of one asleep, and would actually sit down by the road-side and go fast asleep when on her errands of mercy through the South. . . .''

As to the passengers, John Chase was twenty years old, ''chestnut color, of spare build and smart.'' He said that his master, John Campbell Henry, of Cambridge, Maryland, was a ''hard man and that he owned about one hundred and forty slaves.'' Benjamin Ross was described as ''twenty-eight years of age, chestnut color, medium size and shrewd.'' John Ross was ''only twenty-two and had left his wife Harriet Ann . . . and two small children.'' ''Peter Jackson had been hired out to a farmer near Cambridge.'' Catherine (or Jane) was twenty-two and said her master ''was the worst man in the country.'' William Henry Ross was ''thirty-five years of age, of a chestnut color, and well made,'' and said that he had "hardly been treated as well as a gentle-man would treat a dumb brute."

William Still gave them advice "on the subject of temperance, industry, education, etc. Clothing, food and money were also given them to meet their wants, and they were sent on their way rejoicing."

After they left Philadelphia, they were guided to New York city, and then on up through New York state. They arrived in St. Catharines, Canada West, early in January of 1855.

She would help these six people get adjusted to life in St. Catharines, and then in a few more months she would go back to Maryland to help another group of slaves escape. Nothing would ever stop her from helping them, not masters or slave catchers, or overseers or fugitive slave laws.

A Wagon Load of Bricks

FROM 1851 TO 1857, the country moved closer to civil war. During these years Harriet Tubman made eleven trips into Maryland to bring out slaves.

In November, 1856, she rescued Joe Bailey. In the spring she had made two trips to the Eastern Shore. The result of one of these trips is recorded in Still's *Underground Railroad*: "April 1856. The next arrival numbered four passengers, and came under the guidance of 'Moses' (Harriet Tubman) from Maryland. . . ."

The second trip, which took place in May, is mentioned in a letter that Thomas Garrett wrote to J. Miller McKim and William Still of the Philadelphia Vigilance Committee:

Wilmington, 5 mo. 11th, 1856

Esteemed Friends—McKim and Still:—. . . . Those four I wrote thee about arrived safe up in the neighborhood of Longwood, and Harriet Tubman followed after in the stage yesterday. I shall expect five more from the same neighborhood next trip. . . .

As ever your friend,

THOS. GARRETT

The November trip started off inauspiciously. There were three men in the group: Joe Bailey and his brother William, and a man named Peter Pennington. There was one woman, Eliza Nokey.

After Harriet heard Joe's story, her fear of immediate pursuit increased. Joe was a tall, dark man, muscular and handsome. His master had hired him out to another planter, William R. Hughlett, for six years. Finally, Hughlett decided to buy him, for Joe supervised the running of the plantation so well that Hughlett didn't have to pay an overseer. He paid two thousand dollars for Joe.

Joe said the day Hughlett bought him, he beat him with a rawhide, to make certain Joe knew who was the master. Joe told them that he had said to himself, "This is the first and the last time." That night he took a boat and rowed down the river to the plantation where Old Ben lived. He told Ben, "The next time Moses comes, let me know."

The scars on Joe's back weren't healed yet. Harriet worried about that. His height, the bloody stripes on his back, would make it easy to identify him. Perhaps it was the worry, the haste with which they had to move to get away, the fact she felt impelled to urge them to move faster and faster; anyway, her head began to ache. She made them walk along the edge of the road, dangerous, but going through the woods was too slow. As she hurried them along, the scar from the old wound on her temple began to throb like a tooth-ache. The ache in her head increased. She could feel sleep creeping over her like a paralysis. She tried to sing, tried to fight off the sleep, and stumbled, went down on her knees. And was sound asleep.

When she awakened, she had no idea how long she had slept. She heard a man's voice say-ing, ''You've got to trust her. When she has those sleeps you have to leave her alone till she wakes up, she'll wake up pretty soon.''

It was Joe who had spoken. He was squatting on his heels, and Eliza and Bill and Peter were standing up, looking down at her. She was lying flat on the road.

She got to her feet quickly. Her heart seemed to be skipping beats; it was going so fast. They were out in plain sight, all of them; anyone who passed would recognize them for what they were—runaways, fugitives.

She ordered them to follow her and went into the woods that bordered the road, plunging into the woods, almost running. They came behind her, and it seemed to her their footsteps kept pace with the speed of her thoughts: should have been traveling at night, not in broad daylight; should have been concealed, not out in the open like that.

Then she heard them muttering. One of the men said, ''She's taking us back, I can tell, we're going back the same way we come, the woman's crazy—''

She led them on a zigzag course, up a hill and then down. At the foot of the hill there was a small river which followed a winding course. She went straight toward it.

Eliza Nokey said, panic in her voice, ''You goin' wade that?''

Harriet said she had had a dream while she was sleeping. And in the dream she had seen this river.

Eliza said it was too deep to wade, they'd all drown.

Harriet said she was certain there was one place so shallow that they could wade it.

She waded into the stream, water like ice was around her ankles, and as she went forward, it reached her thighs, and then her waist. She turned and looked back, and Joe was the only one who had followed her. The others were standing on the bank watching. Water reached to her shoulders and she kept going. She closed her eyes for a moment, in the grip of a despair as icy cold as the water.

The water began to recede. It was down to her shoulders. But it wasn't the water that was receding, the stream was getting shallower. When the others saw this, they started to wade the river, too. Then all of them reached the opposite bank, dry land, a small island, or neck of land. They were shivering, shocked by the cold, numb, but otherwise unharmed.

The next morning they set out again. They went back the same way they had come, but they did not have to wade through the river. Their host served as guide, and he led them by a long round-about road.

When they reached the spot where Harriet had gone to sleep by the side of the road, the day before, they all shivered. The patrollers had been there, had waited for them there. If they hadn't crossed that river at Harriet's direction, they would have been caught. The evidence was unmistakable: the grass had been trampled by horses' feet; the ground was littered with the stubs of half-smoked cigars.

A poster had been nailed to one of the trees. They recognized it immediately. In the upper left-hand corner there was a woodcut of a black man, a small running figure with a stick over his shoulder, and a bundle tied to the end of the stick, and another stick in his hand.

Harriet tore the poster down, and handed it to Joe. He read it aloud:

HEAVY REWARD

TWO THOUSAND SIX HUNDRED DOLLARS REWARD.—Ran away from the subscriber, on Saturday night, November 15th, 1856, Josiah and William Bailey, and Peter Pennington. Joe is about 5 feet 10 inches in height, of a chestnut color, bald head, with a remarkable scar on one of his cheeks, not positive on which it is, but think it is on the left, under the eye, has intelligent countenance, active, and well-made. He is about 28 years old. Bill is of a darker color, about 5 feet 8 inches in height, stammers a little when confused, well-made, and older than Joe, well dressed, but may have pulled kearsey on over their other clothes. Peter is smaller than either the others, about 25 years of age, dark chestnut color, 5 feet 7 or 8 inches high.

A reward of fifteen hundred dollars will be given to any person who will apprehend the said Joe Bailey, and lodge him safely in the jail at Easton, Talbot Co., Md. and $300 for Bill and $800 for Peter.

> W. R. HUGHLETT,
> John C. Henry,
> T. WRIGHT

When Joe finished reading, there was silence. Harriet tried to say something, and her voice was only a croaking sound in her throat. Again she tried to speak, and couldn't. She must have caught cold from the river. What would she do? Bill sighed. Then Peter groaned.

Eliza Nokey was angry. No one had offered any reward for her return. Then Joe started to sing. He looked at that poster which meant any man who read it would be tempted to start hunting for the slave who was worth fifteen hundred dollars to his master, crumpled it up in his hand, and started to sing.

They hurried in a northerly direction, and Joe kept singing, softly, under his breath.

As they went along, Harriet sensed danger everywhere, smelled danger. They were not safe. She herded them along, sometimes going ahead of them, sometimes walking behind them, prodding them with the butt of the gun. The hoarseness prevented her from speaking.

It was Joe who talked, Joe who encouraged them, Joe who, as if by instinct, told the old stories about the slave ships, the torture, the irons and the whips. When he sang, they moved faster. Eliza Nokey fairly skipped along, as Joe sang.

They saw other places along the road where the patrollers had been, found one place where they must have waited for as much as an hour, in the hope that they would be able to find some trace of this party. The horses had been tied to the trees.

Joe shook his head and stopped singing.

It was daybreak when they reached the outskirts of Wilmington. Within sight of the long
bridge Harriet called a halt. She told the runaways to hide in the woods, not to speak to anyone, not to make a sound, not to move.

She watched the bridge for a long time. It was
guarded. There were posters nailed to the trees all
along the road. Stealthily, cautiously, she took two
of the posters down, and went back to where
she'd left the runaways. Joe said one of the posters was the one he'd read to them before and the
reward for him had been increased to two thousand dollars.

But the other—the little running figure re-
produced on the flimsy paper was that of a
woman. The reward offered for her capture was
twelve thousand dollars. The poster described
her. It said she was dark, short, of a muscular
build, with a deep voice, and that she had a scar
on her left temple, scars on the back of her neck.
Her name was Harriet Tubman. Sometimes she
was called Moses.

Harriet laughed. She said nobody was going to
catch her. She left them again and went as close to
the bridge as she dared, waiting, watching.
Thomas Garrett must know about those posters,
must know the bridge was watched. He would try
to get in touch with her. She was certain of it.

He did. Garrett sent his servant out to look for

Harriet. When Harriet saw him, she signaled to him. They held a conference in the long grass by the side of the road. Then he went back to report to Garrett. Two hours later he was back again with Garrett's message.

It was dark when Harriet returned to the fugitives. As she went toward their hiding place, she signaled her approach by singing:

"Go down, Moses—"

She told them to follow her. She took them through the woods, and then along a road, heavy woods on each side of it, more like a country lane than a road. There was a long wagon there. And men. And the sound of horses, jingle of harness, stamping of feet, soft blowing out of breath.

They got in the wagon, one by one, and lay down flat. Harriet said the men were bricklayers. She said that the men would cover them with bricks. When the men put boards over them, Eliza Nokey made a thin high sound of terror, and Harriet heard her whisper.

The wagon started. There was a sound of hoofbeats. The men on the wagon began to laugh and shout and sing. Then they were on the long bridge and someone cried, "Halt!"

The driver shouted, "Whoa! Whoa!"

When he was asked if he'd seen any runaway Negroes, he laughed and said with that kind of money being offered for them, he planned to start hunting for them as soon as he got home, right after supper.

When they got out of the wagon at Thomas Garrett's house in Wilmington, Garrett said of Harriet, ''She was so hoarse she could hardly speak, and was also suffering with violent tooth-ache.''

Garrett forwarded them to Philadelphia where William Still wrote down their past history in his record book. From Philadelphia they were forwarded to the office of the Antislavery Society in New York.

When they reached New York, it was Joe who lost his courage. The moment they entered the office of Oliver Johnson, head of the New York Antislavery Society, Johnson recognized Joe.

Joe said he wouldn't go any farther because he would be hunted every step of the way, and he couldn't stand it any longer. If a man who had never seen him could recognize him from the description, then the whole dream of freedom was hopeless. He told Harriet to take the others and go on. None of them would be safe as long as he was with them.

But Harriet said they would not go without him. Finally, reluctantly, he went with them.

They were put aboard a train and they passed

through New York state without incident. The conductor had hidden them in the baggage car, but when they approached Niagara Falls, he took them into one of the coaches.

Harriet tried to rouse Joe from his apathy, and urged him to look at Niagara. But he still sat with his head in his hands, refusing to look.

Then she shouted, ''You've crossed the line! You're free, Joe, you're free!''

The others shouted too. Still he sat, bent over, silent. Harriet shook him. ''Joe! Joe! You're a free man!''

Slowly he straightened up in his seat, and then stood up, and lifted his hands, and began to sing.

His voice was like the sound of thunder. Harriet, listening, thought it put a glory over all of them.

19

The Old Folks Go North

IN JUNE OF 1857, Harriet was again working in a hotel in Cape May, New Jersey. While she was there she kept having vivid dreams about Old Rit and Ben, her mother and father. In the dream they were about to be sold. Off and on during the day she would shiver, remembering the sad expression on Old Rit's face.

She had always wanted to bring them North. But she did not know how she could travel with two old people.

It was with a shrug of her shoulders that she started South to get them, thinking that she'd solved all kinds of problems and, with the help of the good Lord, she'd solve this one when she got there. There was an urgency about the dreams that suggested she could waste no time.

She went South by train, counting on the fact that no one would question her because she was

The case of Dred Scott, a slave transported into a free state and then back into a slave state, led to an historic decision by the U.S. Supreme Court in March 1857. Scott was denied his freedom on the grounds that he was not a citizen and therefore unable to sue in court.

going in the wrong direction for a runaway slave. It was broad daylight when she reached Bucktown, Maryland. She deliberately assumed the bent-over posture of an old woman, sidling down the street. She pulled her sunbonnet well over her eyes. There was always the chance she might be recognized because she had lived and worked in and around this area.

She stopped once, at a cabin where a family of free Negroes lived. She bought a pair of fowl from them, and asked that their legs be tied together. As she paid for the chickens she thought it takes a lot of cooking and cleaning and scrubbing to pay for these trips but it's worth it.

When she left Bucktown the chickens were fluttering and squawking and she looked for all the world like an old woman. She was not disguised; it was simply that the bent back and the chickens, legs tied together, transformed her into a granny, obviously coming from or going to market. The chickens would serve to distract the attention of anyone who passed her.

Far down the road she heard the pound, pound, pound of horses' hoofs. She stood still, undecided. Should she hide in the woods? She gathered up her long skirt in one hand, preparing to run. She wouldn't run. Her skirt would be snagged and torn by briars, she might trip and fall. Besides, she still did not know how she was going to get Old Rit and Ben to the North. She might have to take them on a train, and she couldn't ride on a train with her clothing torn, it was one of the earmarks of the fugitive.

As the hoofbeats grew nearer, she pulled her sunbonnet farther down over her face and shortened the length of her steps, edging over to the side of the narrow road, hitching along. When the horse came abreast of her, she looked up, sidewise, at the rider. It was Doc Thompson, her old master, cigar in his mouth.

She gave a hard violent jerk at the string on the chickens' legs, and with a squawk and a wild fluttering of wings, the chickens ran back down the road. Harriet gave a high-pitched, quavering screech and hobbled after them.

Doc Thompson reined in his horse, turned to watch the pursuit. He laughed and then he shouted, ''Go it, Granny! I'll bet on the chickens but go it anyway, Granny! Ha! Ha! Ha!''

She stopped running as soon as she heard him cluck to the horse, and when the hoofbeats started again, she turned and walked purposefully toward the plantation, back straight, head held proudly. She lingered near the edge of the road until it was dark. Then she went toward the quarter, moving so quietly that she was only a shadow that emerged from deeper shadows, disappeared, emerged again. She tapped on the door, lightly.

Slow footsteps approached the door. Old Rit opened the door a little way and said, "Who is it?" caution in her voice.

"It's Hat," Harriet whispered.

Old Rit merely said, "Come in. I didn't think I'd ever see you again."

They stood looking at each other for a moment and then Old Rit hugged Harriet and kissed her. Harriet looked at her mother, frowning, wondering how in the world she was going to make the trip North with her.

If she could get them to Thomas Garrett in Wilmington, everything would be all right. But how get them there? They simply could not walk. Well, if they couldn't walk, they'd have to ride.

She found Dollie Mae lying down under some trees in Barrett's pasture. Someone had left a long rope around her neck. She got the horse up, patted her, talked to her. My, but she's old, she thought. I just hope she'll be able to make the trip.

The stars were out and the air was warm. She got on Dollie's back with difficulty because of the long skirt, and went down the road toward the quarter. True, she had the horse but she needed a wagon and she would need reins of some kind. Well, she'd just have to borrow some things from Doc Thompson. There used to be an old wagon in back of the stable.

She harnessed Dollie up, urged her toward the stable, stopping every once in a while to listen. Nothing. She backed Dollie between the shafts of the old wagon, hurrying now.

Once on the seat she clucked softly. The wagon started moving, creaking faintly as it moved.

She murmured a prayer under her breath when she untied Dollie. Lord, let this horse hold out or we'll never make it.

Then she climbed up on the seat, said, "Giddap," slapped Dollie with the reins and they were off. They traveled all that night. Toward morning, Harriet got off the seat and led Dollie and the wagon off the road. They spent the day in the woods. The old people ate and then went off to sleep. When it got dark they set out again.

Three nights later, just at dusk, Harriet stopped the wagon in front of Thomas Garrett's house in Wilmington. She had got them safely through this far. The rest of the trip would be comparatively easy.

Garrett gave Harriet enough money to take all of them to Canada. From Wilmington on up she followed her usual route, stopping in Philadelphia, and then in New York.

The pattern of her life changed after the rescue of Ben and Old Rit. It was cold in St. Catharines in June, 1857. Old Rit said she did not believe she would ever feel warm again as long as she lived. Ben said nothing. He hugged the fireside and sighed.

She wondered what she ought to do. It wouldn't be safe for them to live in the United States. The Fugitive Slave Law was still in force, though there were few people in the North who would willingly betray a fugitive. Yet it was a risky thing to do.

But she had run risks before, plenty of them. One way or another, she had been running risks all her life. They ought to be fairly safe in New York state. She remembered Auburn, a small town, with elm trees arching over its streets, and smooth lawns, and houses painted white. It was a friendly place.

In 1857 she bought a small frame house in Auburn from William H. Seward, who was at the time the United States Senator from New York. The house was at the end of South Street, beyond the tollgate, on land that belonged to Senator Seward. She had very little money to make a down payment, so there was a rather large mortgage.

That fall she was back in Dorchester County, Maryland, again. In October, William Still recorded the arrival of sixty fugitives from the area in and around Cambridge. All of them had followed the Underground Railroad route under Harriet's direction though she did not go with them all the way to Philadelphia.

But she spent the winter of 1857–58 in St. Catharines, working in the woods, cooking, cleaning, doing whatever jobs she could get.

One day, in April, she went deep into the woods to gather firewood. When she finished, she sat down on a rock to rest. She looked up and saw a man approaching her. In the distance he looked like an old man, his shoulders stooped, but he walked with the swift space-covering gait of a young man.

Then Jarm Loguen came up to them. He told Harriet that the man looking at her with such interest was John Brown, and that he had come a long distance just to meet her and talk with her.

She listened to Brown in silence. He wanted her to tell him the route she had followed on the way North from Maryland, to reveal the hiding places she had used in the swamps, the forests, all the secrets she had learned in the last eight years, in those trips back and forth through the Tidewater country.

He said that he needed this information because he was going to free the slaves, on a large scale. He planned to establish himself in a stronghold in the mountains of Virginia. Once having done that, the slaves would rise up and flock to him. He would arm them with pikes and guns so that they could fight for their freedom. He wanted her to join him in this project so that she could lead the slaves to Canada. He also wanted her to help him here in Canada in raising recruits for the small army of men that he would need for this enterprise.

As he talked she thought of Nat Turner. And she was repelled by the thought of the bloodshed that must inevitably take place, remembering Nat and the bloody swath he had left behind him that night in Virginia, all those years ago, when he too had decided the time had come to free the slaves. This old man, like Nat, worshiped a God of wrath, of vengeance. The God she worshiped was a God of infinite mercy, of gentleness.

Yet his sincerity made a deep impression on her. He was so in earnest. He shared her hatred of slavery, shared her belief that freedom was a right all men should enjoy, and yet—She hesitated.

Finally she said she would help him. Later on,

she suggested a possible date for the beginning of this action—the Fourth of July.

While in St. Catharines, John Brown wrote a letter to his son, John Brown, Jr., reporting on the success of his Canadian trip: "April 8, 1858. . . . I am succeeding to all appearance, beyond my expectation. Harriet Tubman hooked on his [her] whole team at once. He [she] is the most of man, naturally, that I ever met with. There is the most abundant material, and of the right quality, in this quarter, beyond all doubt. . . ."

But Harriet, waiting in St. Catharines, waiting for further word from John Brown, heard nothing.

20

The Lecture Platform

HARRIET SPENT MOST of the winter of 1858–1859 in Boston. She was badly in need of funds. There was the mortgage on the house in Auburn, which she never seemed to be able to pay off, no matter how hard she worked, and she wanted to make another trip to Maryland.

By this time she was known by reputation throughout the North. Many people called her "Molly Pitcher" because of the stories they had heard about the daring rescue trips she made into the South. Her friends in New York had urged her to go to Boston—people there were eager to meet her and equally eager to help her.

Early in December of 1858 she arrived in Boston, with a little packet of letters of introduction and a small bundle of daguerreotypes—pictures of some of her old friends like Gerrit Smith and Thomas Garrett. That afternoon of her arrival she sat in the front parlor of a boarding house waiting for a man named Franklin B. Sanborn. She had never seen him but he knew some of her friends. One of the letters of introduction she had brought from New York was addressed to him.

Then there was a tap on the door of the parlor. She said, "Come in," and stood up, holding herself very straight. The tall man who entered, smiled, said, "Mrs. Tubman?" and when she nodded, said, "I'm Franklin Sanborn."

She did not answer him. Instead she opened the little package of pictures that she had placed on a table near her chair and handed one of them to him. Because it had occurred to her that if he recognized the picture, then surely he was who he said he was—Franklin B. Sanborn. In the back of her mind an old memory flared: the Sims boy, Anthony Burns, Shadrach, all of them arrested here in Boston, charged with being fugitives. And she was a fugitive, too. For all she knew, this big young man smiling at her with such cordiality might be a sheriff—or—

"Do you know who that is?" she asked.

He raised his eyebrows. "It's Gerrit Smith," he said. "Why do you ask?"

When she explained, he nodded, his eyes

amused. "You're quite right to be cautious." As she continued to stand, he said, "Let's sit down and talk."

He sat down beside her, asked her a few questions, listened intently as she answered, kept her talking—for more than an hour. As he was leaving he asked her if she would make a speech at an antislavery meeting in about two weeks. At first she refused. But he overrode her objections, saying, "You have no idea how important it is that you should tell some of these stories to the people here in Boston."

Two weeks later there she was on the platform at Faneuil Hall. She was wearing a dark gray long-skirted cotton dress. The only adornment was a bit of lace at the neck and jet buttons down the front. She held an old black reticule on her lap. The other speakers were distinguished-looking men: Wendell Phillips, Franklin Sanborn, Thomas Wentworth Higginson.

When Sanborn introduced her, she stood looking shyly at this audience of well-dressed people, not knowing what to say. And someone on the platform asked her a question, and then another. Then she started talking, telling about the trips she had made back into the slave country, how she carefully selected the slaves that would go

North with her, how they traveled mostly on foot, wading through rivers, hiding in haystacks, in barns.

She described the rest of the journey, the stop at Thomas Garrett's in Wilmington, and the slow journey North to Philadelphia, where William Still recorded their names and the names of their owners in his thick notebook.

This firsthand information about the Underground Railroad, by a woman who had served as one of its conductors, thrilled that first audience before whom she spoke. They stood on their feet and cheered and clapped when she finished.

After that first speech she was a much sought-after speaker in Boston and its environs. Her appearance had undergone subtle changes during the course of the years. There was something brooding and tender in her face, a gentleness in her eyes. The lips were slightly compressed, the only indication of a never quite fulfilled hunger for affection. Her speaking voice, deep in pitch, slightly husky, was more beautiful than ever. Yet sometimes she sat on a platform in plain sight of an audience and went sound asleep just as she had often done on the long road to the North. In spite of this strange handicap, she was a tremendously successful public speaker.

During that winter in Boston, she saw John

Brown several times. He called himself Captain Smith because he did not want his enemies to know his whereabouts. Harriet told him all she knew of the routes to the North, the hiding places on the way out of Maryland, drawing crude maps for him. During the spring and early summer she waited for further word from him, and heard nothing more.

She was much in demand as a speaker. She visited Concord, Framingham, Worcester, speaking at antislavery meetings.

Early in June, Thomas Wentworth Higginson told her that he had had a letter from Franklin Sanborn. And that Sanborn had said John Brown ''is desirous of getting someone to go to Canada and collect recruits for him among the fugitives . . . with H. [Harriet] Tubman, or alone. . . .''

Higginson told her that he had lost confidence in the plan. He said that it had ''grown rather vague and dubious'' in his mind because of the repeated postponements.

Harriet did not know what to think. The Fourth of July had come and gone. On that day she made a speech at a meeting of the Massachusetts Anti-Slavery Society at Framingham. Someone said that Brown was in Maryland, and someone else said, no, he was in New York.

On the 1st of August she was back in Boston to

make another speech. She liked Boston. Whenever she had a moment's leisure she went to Boston Common. Sanborn had told her something of its history, said that years ago a Quaker, a woman, had been hanged there and that a mob once tried to hang William Lloyd Garrison there. Sanborn said that these days all manner of people aired their grievances on Boston Common. He spoke of Amelia Bloomer, and laughed, describing the costume she had worn when she made a speech there one afternoon. She had on full, stiff trousers that reached all the way to her ankles and were tied there. He said it was one of the funniest sights he'd ever seen.

Harriet thought that over, and though she did not say so, decided that she could have used just such a costume many times. Long, full skirts would hamper any woman who had walked and ridden along a road that almost ran under the ground.

Harriet never heard from John Brown again, never saw him again. She was unaware of the fact that Brown and his assistants kept referring to her in the letters that they sent to the Boston Abolitionists who were helping to finance his project. ''Harriet Tubman is probably in New Bedford, sick. She has staid in N.E. [New England] a long time. And been a kind of missionary." "I have sent a note to Harriet requesting her to come to Boston." "When Harriet comes. . . .''

But Harriet never came. Perhaps she was ill, perhaps Higginson had told her that he had lost confidence in the plan, perhaps word of Frederick Douglass's absolute refusal to enter what he believed to be a steel trap had influenced her—in any event, she was not at Harper's Ferry, nor did she send any recruits from Canada.

On October 17, 1859, she was in New York, visiting friends. It had been years since she had experienced that curious fluttering sensation of her heart, a wild beating inside her chest, that she interpreted as a warning of danger.

No argument could shake off her feeling of disaster. Later in the day they heard that the United States Government Arsenal at Harper's Ferry had been seized. The next day's papers carried the news: eighteen men in the fire-engine house with Brown, ten of them were killed, including two of Brown's sons. John Brown had been taken prisoner.

A week later, Old John Brown was put on trial. He was found guilty and sentenced to death.

Harriet was deeply affected by Brown's death. She worshiped his memory. It seemed to her amazing that a white man, free, independent, should have held such strong convictions on the subject of slavery that he was willing to risk his life in order that slaves should be free.

Someone read her the final statement that he made. She had it read to her over and over again, until she knew parts of it by heart: ''. . . I say I am yet too young to understand that God is any respecter of persons. . . . I believe that to have interfered as I have done, as I have always freely admitted I have done, in behalf of His despised poor, I did no wrong but right. . . .''

Harriet always regretted that he had not made his plans more carefully. The slaves in the area had no knowledge of his intention, had been given not so much as a hint that such a plan existed, or that it in any way involved them, and they were as disturbed and frightened by the action at Harper's Ferry as the rest of the country.

She resolved to do something in memory of Captain John Brown, something, she did not know what, ''in behalf of God's despised poor.''

21

With the Union Army

AFTER THE DEATH of John Brown, Harriet began to feel dissatisfied with the life she was leading. It seemed to her that she was doing absolutely nothing for the cause of freedom. Certainly the audiences before whom she spoke offered no challenge to her ingenuity or her imagination.

She was still surprised by the enthusiastic reception she was accorded. When she finished talking, people began to clap, and then they stood and cheered, and came up to the platform to shake hands with her, to give her money. Many of them told her not to make any more trips into the South for fear she would be caught.

This was a thought that she impatiently rejected as of no consequence. She was more interested in how the whole question of slavery would be settled. She was certain that it would be settled soon—one way or another. Southerners believed that the entire North had supported John Brown and in 1860 they lived in dread because they thought that a tremendous uprising of the slaves might still occur. Northerners, as far as she could tell from what she saw and heard in her travels, had turned the Fugitive Slave Law into a joke. People said that in northern Ohio, where Levi Coffin operated the busiest branch of the Underground Railroad, it was impossible to put an Abolitionist in jail and keep him there, no matter how guilty he might be of harboring runaways.

It was almost impossible to try a runaway slave. She found that out herself, because she became involved in the case of a runaway slave who had been arrested and was to be tried.

On April 27, 1860, she was in Troy, New York. She had spent the night there and was going on to Boston to attend an antislavery meeting. That morning she was on her way to the railroad station. She walked along the street slowly. She never bothered to find out when a train was due, she simply sat in the station and waited until a train came which was going in the direction she desired.

She stopped walking to watch a crowd of people in front of the courthouse, a pushing, shoving, shouting crowd. She wondered what had happened. A fight? An accident?

Harriet started working her way through the crowd, elbowing a man, nudging a woman. Now and then she asked a question. She learned that a runaway slave named Charles Nalle had been arrested and was being taken inside the court-house to be tried.

When she finally got close enough to see the runaway's face, a handsome frightened face, his guards had forced him up the courthouse steps. They were trying to get through the door but people blocked the way.

She knew a kind of fury against the system, against the men who would force this man back into slavery when they themselves were free. The Lord did not intend that people should be slaves, she thought. Then without even thinking, she went up the steps, forced her way through the crowd, until she stood next to Nalle.

There was a small boy standing near her, mouth open, eyes wide with curiosity. She grabbed him by the collar and whispered to him fiercely, ''You go out in the street and holler 'Fire, fire' as loud as you can.''

The crowd kept increasing and she gave a nod of satisfaction. That little boy must have got out there in the street and must still be hollering that there's a fire. She bent over, making her shoulders droop, bending her back in the posture of an old

woman. She pulled her sunbonnet way down, so
that it shadowed her face. Just in time, too. Suddenly she shouted, "Don't let them take him!
Don't let them take him!"

She attacked the nearest policeman so suddenly that she knocked him down. She wanted to
laugh at the look of surprise on his face when he
realized that the mumbling old woman who had
stood so close to him had suddenly turned into a
creature of vigor and violence. Grabbing Nalle by
the arm, she pulled him along with her, forcing
her way down the steps, ignoring the blows she
received, not really feeling them, taking pleasure
in the fact that in all these months of inactivity she
had lost none of her strength.

When they reached the street they were both
knocked down. Harriet snatched off her bonnet
and tied it on Nalle's head. When they stood up it
was impossible to pick him out of the crowd.
People in the street cleared a path for them,
helped hold back the police. As they turned off
the main street, they met a man driving a horse
and wagon. He reined in the horse.

Nalle was rapidly driven to Schenectady and
from there he went on to the West—and safety.

Harriet's friends knew that she was in danger
of arrest for the part she had played in Nalle's

rescue. They saw to it that she stayed hidden in a house on the outskirts of Troy for two days.

Shortly afterward she went to Boston where she filled two speaking engagements, one at a meeting of the New England Antislavery Society on May 27th, the other at a women's suffrage meeting on the 1st of June.

After this she returned to Auburn, where she spent the summer. She was restless, impatient. People were talking about Abe Lincoln. He had won the Republican nomination for the presidency in the spring. No one thought he had a chance of winning the election. Even if he did, Harriet doubted that he would do anything about slavery.

In November, 1860, she made another trip to Tidewater Maryland. On December 1st, Thomas Garrett wrote one of his characteristic letters to William Still in Philadelphia:

> I write to let thee know that Harriet Tubman is again in these parts. She arrived last evening from one of her trips of mercy to God's poor, bringing two men with her as far as New Castle. I agreed to pay a man last evening, to pilot them on their way to Chester county; the wife of one of the men, with two or three children, was left some thirty miles below, and I gave Harriet ten dollars, to hire a man with carriage, to take them to Chester county. She said a man had offered for that

sum, to bring them on. I shall be very uneasy about them, till I hear they are safe. There is now much more risk on the road, till they arrive here, than there has been for several months past, as we find that some poor, worthless wretches are constantly on the look out on two roads, that they cannot well avoid more especially with carriage, yet, as it is Harriet who seems to have had a special angel to guard her on her journey of mercy, I have hope.

Thy Friend,
Thomas Garrett

Despite Garrett's uneasiness, the entire party arrived safely in Philadelphia. William Still wrote their names down on loose slips of paper. His big notebook had been hidden, for ''the capture of John Brown's papers and letters, with names and plans in full, admonished us that such papers and correspondence as had been preserved concerning the Underground Rail Road, might perchance be captured by a pro-slavery mob.''

Still wrote swiftly and briefly: ''Arrival from Dorchester Co., 1860,'' and under it, ''Harriet Tubman's Last 'Trip' to Maryland.'' Then he put down the names of the people who came with her, and that was all.

When Harriet returned from this trip, her friends in Auburn hurried her off to Canada, suddenly afraid for her safety. It was not until she reached Canada that she learned that Old Abe Lincoln had won the election in November.

In December, South Carolina seceded from the Union. As the year turned, the cotton states began leaving the Union: Mississippi, Florida, Alabama, Georgia, Louisiana, Texas.

In January, 1861, she was back in Boston. She was there when John A. Andrew was inaugurated Governor of Massachusetts. He was a short heavy-set man who wore spectacles. Men said he was a Free Soiler and a radical. The day he was inaugurated, he sent out a call for the Massachusetts Militia, and sent a man to England to see about guns.

In February, the states that had seceded formed a new union called the Confederate States of America. Jefferson Davis was elected President of the Confederacy. On April 14th, the Confederacy took over Fort Sumter. Lincoln sent out a call for militia.

Governor John A. Andrew of Massachusetts telegraphed the President, ''The quota of troops required of Massachusetts is ready. How will you have them proceed?'' The answer was, ''Send them by rail.''

No other state in the Union was prepared to act so quickly. In a week's time, Massachusetts was able to send out infantry, riflemen and artillery, properly equipped and thoroughly drilled.

It was John Andrew, who was responsible for

Harriet Tubman's final major role. During the Civil War she became a scout, a spy, a nurse for the Union forces. In May, 1862, she boarded the *Atlantic*, a Government transport, headed for Beaufort, which is located on Port Royal, one of the Sea Islands, off the coast of South Carolina. She was sent there at the recommendation of Governor Andrew.

The Confederate forts had been taken on November 7, 1861, and Port Royal and St. Helena were being used by the Union Army as supply stations. Slaves had been flocking to these islands ever since the Union forces had set up headquarters there. These slaves were referred to as "contrabands." The term originated from an army report of May 24, 1861. Three fugitives were brought into Fortress Monroe by the Union picket guard. The Confederates asked for their rendition under the terms of the Fugitive Slave Law, but they were informed by General Butler that "under the peculiar circumstances, he considered the fugitives 'contraband' of war."

Port Royal was filled with contrabands, poverty-stricken, sick, homeless, starving. A hospital had been set up for them on Port Royal.

It was in this contraband hospital that Harriet Tubman began to play her new role of nurse. She said, "I'd go to the hospital, I would, early every morning. I'd get a big chunk of ice, I would, and put it in a basin, and fill it with water; then I'd take a sponge and begin. First man I'd come to, I'd thrash away the flies, and they'd rise, they would, like bees around a hive. Then I'd begin to bathe the wounds, and by the time I bathed off three or four, the fire and heat would have melted the ice and made the water warm, and it would be as red as clear blood. Then I'd go and get more ice, I would, and by the time I got to the next ones, the flies would be around the first ones black and thick as ever.''

More deadly than the wounds was the dysentery. Each morning when she went back to the hospital, she found more and more people had died from it. She was certain she could check it if she could find the same roots and herbs here on the island that had grown in Maryland. But this was a strange new country to her; even the plant life was different.

One night she went into a wooded area, near the water, and searched until she found the great white flowers of the water lily floating on the surface, reached down and pulled up the roots, hunted until she found crane's bill. Then she went back to the small house where she lived and boiled the roots and herbs, making a strange dark-looking concoction. It was a bitter-tasting brew. But it worked. The next morning she gave it to a man who was obviously dying, and slowly he got better.

Once again men called her Moses, saying that no one could die if Moses was at the bedside.

In January, 1863, shortly after Lincoln had proclaimed the slaves free, she saw a regiment of Negro soldiers for the first time. Thomas Wentworth Higginson, their commanding officer, was an old friend of Harriet's. As Harriet watched these men parade through the sandy streets, shaded by the tremendous live oaks, one thousand ex-slaves marching in unison, she was overcome by emotion. The band of the Eighth Maine met the regiment at the entrance to Beaufort and escorted them all the way.

She thought this the most moving sight she had ever beheld: a regiment of black, newly freed South Carolinians wearing the uniform of the Union forces, escorted by the band of a white regiment. She knew how Sergeant Prince Rivers, the six-foot color sergeant of the First Carolina Volunteers, felt when he said, ''And when that band wheel in before us, and march on—my God! I quit this world altogether.''

About a month later, she started serving as a scout for Colonel James Montgomery, who had encamped at Port Royal with the first detachment of the Second South Carolina Volunteers, also composed of ex-slaves. On the night of June 2, 1863, Harriet accompanied Montgomery and his men in a raid up the Combahee River. They had two objectives: to destroy or take up the torpedoes that the enemy had placed in the Combahee and to bring back to Port Royal as many contrabands as they could entice away from the river area.

They soon found out that they would not have to entice the inhabitants away. As the gunboats went farther and farther up the Combahee, they began to see slaves working in the rice fields. At first the slaves ran away, toward the woods. Then the word was passed around, "Lincoln's gunboats done come to set us free."

People started coming toward the boats, coming down the paths, through the meadows, for on each side of the river there were rice fields and slaves working in them. They kept coming, with bundles on their heads, children riding on their mothers' shoulders, all of them ragged, dirty, the children naked.

They were taken off the shore in rowboats. All the contrabands tried to get in the small boats at once. Even after the boats were crowded, they clung to the sides of them, holding them fast to the shore. The men rowing the boats struck at their hands with the oars, but they would not let go. They were afraid they would be left behind.

Finally Montgomery shouted from the deck of one of the gunboats, "Moses, you'll have to give 'em a song."

Harriet sang:

Of all the whole creation in the East or in the West,
The glorious Yankee nation is the greatest and the best.
Come along! Come along! don't be alarmed,
Uncle Sam is rich enough to give you all a farm.

As each verse ended, the contrabands threw up their hands and shouted, "Glory! Glory! Glory!" Immediately the small boats pulled off. Hurriedly unloading their passengers on the decks of the gunboats, they came back and got more. After the small boats were filled, Harriet had to sing again and again until they got all 750 contrabands on board.

Shortly afterward, Harriet had someone write a letter to Franklin B. Sanborn in Boston, asking for a bloomer dress because long skirts were a handicap on an expedition.

Sanborn was at that time editor of *The Boston Commonwealth*. He made a front-page story of the Combahee raid, and Harriet's part in it. It appeared Friday, July 10, 1863: "Col. Montgomery and his gallant band of 300 black soldiers, under the guidance of a black woman, dashed into the enemy's country, struck a bold and effective blow . . . and brought off near 800 slaves. . . .''

"Since the rebellion she [Harriet] has devoted herself to her great work of delivering the bond-man, with an energy and sagacity that cannot be exceeded. Many and many times she has penetrated the enemy's lines and discovered their situation and condition, and escaped without injury, but not without extreme hazard. . . .''

22

The Last Years

IN THE SPRING OF 1864, Harriet went back to Auburn
to rest, to visit with Old Rit and Ben. She had
been with the Military Department of the South
for two years.

Harriet stayed in Auburn for a year. During the
summer she paid a visit to Boston. The following
spring she was in Washington, for she intended to
return to Port Royal. She even received a War
Department order providing for transportation
there, dated at Washington, March 20, 1865:
"Pass Mrs. Harriet Tubman (colored) to Hilton
Head and Charleston, S.C., with free transportation on a Gov't transport. By order of Sec. of
War." This was signed by Louis H. Pelonge,
"Asst. Agt. Gener'l." But instead of returning to
the Department of the South, she worked in the
Contraband Hospital at Fortress Monroe. She was
there when the war ended on April 9, 1865.

On April 2nd, Grant took Petersburg. A week later, April 9th, Lee surrendered to him at Appomattox Courthouse.

Six nights after Lee's surrender, Lincoln was shot by John Wilkes Booth. He died the next morning, April 15, 1865.

Harriet stayed at Fortress Monroe until July of 1865. Then she went back to Auburn, New York. The war had been over nearly four months. She was tired. Old Rit and Ben needed her.

With the ratification of the Thirteenth Amendment to the Constitution in December, the long period of agitation for the abolition of slavery came to an end. Like many others who in one way or another had worked toward that goal, Harriet was at a loss as to what to do next. She sought for a new cause, and never really found one. Like many other former Abolitionists, she became interested in the movement for women's suffrage. She helped raise money for schools for the newly freed slaves. She farmed a little, raising fruit and vegetables, looked after Old Rit and Ben, and offered food and shelter to any homeless wanderer who needed a place to stay. She made repeated efforts to obtain some kind of remuneration for her service with the Union forces. Her friends wrote letters for her, presented petitions to Congressional committees—and nothing came of it.

One day in October, 1867, she learned of the death of John Tubman to whom she had been married. He was murdered in Talbot County, Maryland, on the road to Airey.

When she heard of John's death, she felt old and lonely. True, the people in Auburn liked her, admired her. They knew she had little or no money, had to support her old parents as best she could, knew that she could never turn away from her door anyone who said that he had no home, needed food, needed help, and so always had a larger household than one woman could hope to feed and clothe. The neighbors brought food to the little house on South Street—a bag of flour, a sack of potatoes, or a basket of apples. Friendly people.

In May of 1868, one of Harriet's friends and admirers, Mrs. Sarah Hopkins Bradford, a school-teacher who lived in Auburn, decided to do something to raise some money for her. She began to write the story of Harriet's life. Most of the direct quotations used by biographers of Harriet Tubman are possible only because of Mrs. Bradford, who first recorded them.

Mrs. Bradford's book, *Scenes in the Life of Harriet Tubman*, appeared early in 1869. On January 9th

Harriet Tubman (far right) is pictured here in the late 1890s *with her second husband and some of her followers.*

The Boston Commonwealth, in announcing its publication, said that the proceeds from the sale of the biography were to go to Harriet.

She received twelve hundred dollars from the sale of the book. She paid off the mortgage on her house, for she was still in debt to Senator Seward for it. She even had money left over afterward.

But she regretted that it came too late for Ben and Old Rit. They were both dead by then.

In March of that year, she married again. Her husband, Nelson Davis, was more than twenty years younger than she. The folk in Auburn said Harriet had married him in order to take care of him, that even though he was a big, handsome, young man, he had tuberculosis.

True or not, he was obviously unable to contribute to the support of the household on South Street where he lived with Harriet. The supply of money there never wholly met the need for it. And so, in 1886, Mrs. Bradford came to Harriet's rescue for the second time. She wrote another small volume about Harriet, entitled *Harriet, the Moses of Her People*. Again any money from the book was to go to Harriet, who now wanted to found a home for the aged and infirm.

Nelson Davis died on October 14, 1888. He was forty-four years old. Though Harriet had repeatedly applied for a pension for herself or back pay to reimburse her for those years she had served with the Union forces, her claim was never allowed. But in 1899 she was awarded a pension of twenty dollars a month, not for her own services, but as "the widow of Nelson Davis, who served in Company G, Eighth United States Infantry, from September 1863, to November 1865, and was honorably discharged.''

As she grew older, the pattern of her life changed again. Finally, she became a tiny little old woman, peddling vegetables from door to door in Auburn. She didn't make many stops in the course of a day. There wasn't time. At each house, she was invited inside, told to sit down, and urged to tell a story about some phase of her life.

It was as the storyteller, the bard, that Harriet's active years came to a close. She had never learned to read and write. She compensated for this handicap by developing a memory on which was indelibly stamped everything she had ever heard or seen or experienced. She had a highly developed sense of the dramatic, a sense of the comic, and because in her early years she had memorized verses from the Bible, word for word, the surge and sway of the majestic rhythm of the King James version of the Bible was an integral part of her speech. It was these qualities that made her a superb storyteller.

She could speak of the death of Lincoln, and epitomize all the sorrow in the world by telling about an old man, at the Contraband Hospital at Fortress Monroe, who, hearing that Lincoln was dead, lifted his tremulous old voice in prayer: ''We kneel upon the ground, with our faces in our hands, and our hands in the dust, and cry to Thee for mercy, O Lord, this evening.''

Sometimes she talked about Old John Brown, the man with the hawk's face and the white beard, and the fanatic's eyes, cold and hard as granite. She told about the time Old Brown took her to see Wendell Phillips and when he introduced her, he said, ''Mr. Phillips, I bring you one of the bravest people on this continent—*General Tubman, as we call her.*''

Then again she spoke of Port Royal and the contrabands, and the strange speech of the Gullahs of South Carolina, and told about how they had said their masters had told them the Yankees had hoofs, horns and tails, and would sell them to Cuba, how they called the Confederates *secesh buckra* (white men who were secessionists). She showed her passes, those precious pieces of paper that she could not read though she knew by heart what each one of them said, a little bundle of much-fingered, well-worn paper, many of the documents barely decipherable they had been handled so much.

Harriet and her one-woman audience were no longer in a quiet kitchen in the North; they were in cypress swamps, or walking under live oaks hung with Spanish moss that waved like gray drapery overhead; they saw cotton fields and rice fields, and heard the swash of a river against the banks, and listened to the aching sweetness of a mockingbird, on an island where an incredible moon turned night into day.

Sometimes she went even farther back in her memory, to the days of the plantation and the overseer and the master. Then her listener could see a row of sway-backed cabins, smell the smoky smell from the fireplaces, could see a fifteen-year-old girl huddled under a dirty blanket, could see the great hole in her head and blood pouring from what should have been a mortal wound.

Whoever heard her talk like that had a deeper understanding of the long hard way she had come, had a deeper understanding of what lay behind Gettysburg and Appomattox.

In 1903 she turned her home and twenty-five acres of land over to the African Methodist Episcopal Zion Church of Auburn, to be used as a home for the sick, the poor, the homeless, though she continued to live there herself. She wanted it called the John Brown Home. But shortly afterward, she expressed her dissatisfaction about the way the home was being conducted.

Harriet, who to the end of her life retained that rarest of human virtues, compassion, said: "When I give the Home over to Zion Church, what do you suppose they did? Why, they made a rule that nobody should come in without a hundred dollars. Now I wanted to make a rule that nobody could come in unless they had no money. What's the good of a Home if a person who wants to get in has to have money?"

She died on March 10, 1913. Of her old friends and associates, only Sanborn and Higginson were still alive. The others had gone long before: Theodore Parker, Thomas Garrett, William H. Seward, William Lloyd Garrison, Frederick Douglass, Colonel James Montgomery.

In many ways she represented the end of an era, the most dramatic, and the most tragic, era in American history. Despite her work as a nurse, a scout, and a spy, in the Civil War, she will be remembered longest as a conductor on the Underground Railroad, the railroad to freedom.

On July 12, 1914, the city of Auburn paid tribute to her. During the day flags were flown at half-staff. At night a tremendous mass meeting was held in the Auditorium, where a bronze tablet which had been inscribed to her memory was

Harriet Tubman (ca. 1821–1913): "With rare courage she led over three hundred Negroes up from slavery to freedom. . . ."

unveiled. The tablet was placed on the front entrance of the Courthouse in Auburn. This is what it says:

IN MEMORY OF HARRIET TUBMAN.
BORN A SLAVE IN MARYLAND ABOUT 1821.
DIED IN AUBURN, N.Y., MARCH 10TH, 1913.
CALLED THE MOSES OF HER PEOPLE,
DURING THE CIVIL WAR. WITH RARE
COURAGE SHE LED OVER THREE HUNDRED
NEGROES UP FROM SLAVERY TO FREEDOM,
AND RENDERED INVALUABLE SERVICE
AS NURSE AND SPY.
WITH IMPLICIT TRUST IN GOD
SHE BRAVED EVERY DANGER AND
OVERCAME EVERY OBSTACLE. WITHAL
SHE POSSESSED EXTRAORDINARY
FORESIGHT AND JUDGMENT SO THAT
SHE TRUTHFULLY SAID
"ON MY UNDERGROUND RAILROAD
I NEBBER RUN MY TRAIN OFF DE TRACK
AN' I NEBBER LOS' A PASSENGER."
THIS TABLET IS ERECTED
BY THE CITIZENS OF AUBURN.

For Further Reading

Bisson, Terry. *Harriet Tubman: Anti-Slavery Activist*. New York: Chelsea House, 1989.

Smith, Kathie. *Harriet Tubman*. New York: Messner, 1989.

Sterling, Dorothy. *Freedom Train: The Story of Harriet Tubman*. New York: Scholastic, 1987.

Index

13.95   condition noted 3/20